HELP! THE SMARTPHONE ATE MY FAMILY

HELP! THE SMARTPHONE ATE MY FAMILY

A Parent's Survival Guide for the Digital Age

Phillip Telfer

www.MediaTalk101.org

www.phillLiptelfer.com
Facebook @PhillipTelferAuthor
YouTube @philliptelfermusic
X @PhillipTelfer

Help! The Smartphone Ate My Family
Copyright © 2025 by Phillip Telfer

Published by Media Talk 101
www.mediatalk101.org
Facebook @MediaTalk101
YouTube @MediaTalk101
X @MediaTalk101

All rights reserved. No portion of this book may be reproduced, stored in a retrieval system, or transmitted in any form or by any means—electronic, mechanical, photocopy, recording, scanning, or other—except for brief quotations in critical reviews or articles, without the prior written permission of the publisher.

Unless noted otherwise, Scripture taken from the New King James Version®. Copyright © 1982 by Thomas Nelson, Inc. Used by permission. All rights reserved.

Scriptures marked as (GNB) are taken from the Good News Bible – Second Edition © 1992 by American Bible Society.

Scripture quotations marked (NASB) are taken from the NEW AMERICAN STANDARD BIBLE®, Copyright ©1960, 1962, 1963, 1968, 1971, 1972, 1973, 1975, 1977, 1995 by The Lockman Foundation. Used by permission.

Scripture quotations marked (ESV) are from the ESV® Bible (The Holy Bible, English Standard Version®), copyright © 2001 by Crossway, a publishing ministry of Good News Publishers. Used by permission. All rights reserved.

Scripture quotations marked (NIV) are taken from the Holy Bible, New International Version®, NIV®. Copyright © 1973, 1978, 1984, 2011 by Biblica, Inc.™ Used by permission of Zondervan. All rights reserved worldwide. www.zondervan.com The "NIV" and "New International Version" are trademarks registered in the United States Patent and Trademark Office by Biblica, Inc.™

ISBN 979-8-9998558-0-0 (Paperback)
ISBN 979-8-9998558-1-7 (Hardbound)
ISBN 979-8-9998558-2-4 (eBook)

TABLE OF CONTENTS

Chapter 1: Help! The Smartphone Ate My Family..........................1
Chapter 2: Can the Smartphone be Tamed?........................7
Chapter 3: Health Foods and Goat Yoga...........................15
Chapter 4: Neither Technophobe Nor Technophile 21
Chapter 5: The Great Digital Migration 27
Chapter 6: Why Do We Give Our Children Smartphones? 31
Chapter 7: Driver's Ed 41
Chapter 8: My Children as Guinea Pigs..........................57
Chapter 9: Ten Tips for Taming Tech 67
Chapter 10: Who Needs Sleep? 85
Chapter 11: The Suffocation of Social Media......................95
Chapter 12: The Suffocation of Social Media: Part 2 105
Chapter 13: The Dark Side of Screen Time 113
Chapter 14: The Dark Side of Screen Time: Pornography..............119
Chapter 15: The Dark Side of Screen Time: Girls' Body Image.....131
Chapter 16: The Dark Side of Screen Time: User-Generated Content, Sextortion, Predators, and Action Steps......141
Chapter 17: Battling Boredom 149
Chapter 18: Time Matters.......................................161
Chapter 19: Tools or Toys? 169
Chapter 20: Restoring the Soul of Your Family in the Digital Age...177
Chapter 21: Handle With Care 193
Appendix A: Parent's Guide to Parental Control Apps 205
Appendix B: Parent's Guide to Porn Accountability Apps............211
Author Page: About the Author...................................217
Extras: Free Resources from Media Talk 101 218

CHAPTER 1

HELP! THE SMARTPHONE ATE MY FAMILY

The 1984 film *Gremlins*, appropriately categorized as a comedy horror, tells the tale of a cute but mysterious creature. The fictitious animal is given to a young man named Billy as a present from his dad, who also passes along some warnings. This unusual but adorable creature must be governed by three strict rules or else it will become a problem. More than a problem!

Unfortunately, Billy doesn't follow the strict rules, and the story takes a dark turn when the creature begins to multiply. The additional creatures mischievously trick Billy into breaking another one of the strict rules and they end up morphing into destructive little monsters. They wreak havoc on the entire town, terrorizing and even killing people.

Like the story of Gremlins, many parents today are giving their children a seemingly cute and mysterious pet called the smartphone. The initial enthusiasm for the smartphone often wears off when problems start to arise. Like the story of *Gremlins*, these technological wonders start out seemingly innocent, but they can quickly morph into monsters that threaten to devour your children. In fact, it's not just the children being consumed, nearly every member of the family is in jeopardy.

Like all good stories, we hope for a good ending, not just a tragic tale of loss and destruction. A small group of friends and family in the movie *Gremlins* overcome the little monsters in the end. In this book, I hope to encourage you to join a growing number of parents who are forging a path in this digital age with wisdom and 21st century savvy. Children today need help. Teens need help. They need your help, but you might by thinking, "I need help!" We are all navigating in uncharted waters.

Toddlers and teens alike have entered a world that didn't exist twenty years ago. Predecessors of smartphones, such as the Blackberry, existed before the first iPhone hit the market in 2007, but very few would disagree that the modern smartphone revolution began to take flight when the iPhone hit the market, followed afterwards by new Android devices. The world is forever changed; parenting is forever changed.

Maybe you're realizing, like many others, that your family is out of balance and losing focus. Very few people these days will argue with the fact that screen time has become an increasing problem in their personal lives and in their families, but many don't know how to set a better trajectory. You might be wondering, "How will reading this book benefit me or my family?" Great question!

I want to help you and your family find balance and regain focus. You'll learn how you can benefit spiritually, emotionally, physically, and socially as you handle smartphones and other technologies with wisdom and discipline. Youth and adults alike need help with learning how to handle digital tools in a way that is beneficial rather than detrimental to personal wellbeing and relationships. This book will equip you with helpful tools for carefully navigating today's digital landscape.

We have so many amazing digital tools today that provide tremendous benefit, meaningful connections, and productivity. But many people feel like their lives are becoming controlled by technology, instead of technology being under their control.

The control over our lives by our digital tools has resulted in a variety of problems including loneliness, depression, anxiety, the fear of missing out, and purpose and identity problems to name a few. A person's social experience is not necessarily richer or deeper for all the digital interaction, and many are starting to realize that relationships are becoming shallow and artificial because of it. Today's connectivity is not necessarily drawing us closer to one another; instead, we are feeling farther apart.

Smartphones are disruptive in many ways to children and teens. We will look at the emerging problems and take note of good things children are missing out on because of a screen-based culture. This generation has experienced the explosive growth of new technologies and innovative digital platforms. Yet, we haven't had the education, the media literacy training, to keep pace with all the rapid changes.

This book will not only help identify the problems but also point you to solutions, to helpful action steps, to answers for common questions that are being pondered. You'll learn why your worldview matters, how to battle boredom, and how to keep from being suffocated by social media.

You'll benefit from learning how to develop healthy convictions and make good decisions based on Biblical principles and help keep your children from being cheated out of the life that God wants them to live. You'll learn about the positives and negatives of the digital tools at your fingertips as well as some tips and tricks to help you succeed.

I want to help you understand why it is important for you to have value-based goals that can motivate you to set realistic expectations. You'll learn how to develop good habits and self-control as you establish a healthy media diet in your daily life.

I've personally read many books on this subject, but very few are written from a Christian perspective. In other books, you can learn about the data from studies or read sensational stories to make you fearful or learn about the problems of technology without dealing with the problems in our hearts. The subject of your child's soul is certainly a critical factor if you are truly searching for solutions. With all the noise, the distractions, and convenient means for escapism, many feel distant from God and question the possibility of experiencing anything differently. Learn how media choices may be affecting your family's spiritual life and how to break through the digital distractions to see God more clearly.

Let me paint a picture for you of what this could look like if you take to heart the lessons in this book. The scene portrays parents helping their children thrive in the digital age by utilizing the tools in beneficial ways and at appropriate ages.

Your children need guidance on how to keep from going overboard on entertainment and how to moderate their elective time. I hope this book will be a catalyst for you to help blaze a trail for this generation and demonstrate what it looks like to regain focus and find balance in your life when it comes to entertainment, media, and technology.

Most importantly, in this book you'll receive encouragement to fix your eyes on Jesus and have a real and growing relationship with Him. Your relationship with Christ can help you maintain healthy tech and media habits that won't undermine your physical, emotional, mental, social, and spiritual health.

Now for what this book cannot help you with. This book does not cover the possible underlying problems between parents and their children that may have nothing to do with media or technology. Parenting has always been hard, long before smartphones, 5G, Netflix, or Xbox 360. Problems have stemmed from sinful hearts since the first family.

Brokenness in homes is heartbreaking, and many helpful books have been written with the hope of healing. If there is a problem in your home besides problems with smartphones, it may be something to prioritize before tackling this subject. On the other hand, smartphones are becoming a major instigator of brokenness in teens and their families and other relationships. Careless use of today's technologies often amplifies existing problems that can go from bad to worse. Getting a grip on technology in your home, however, may not be the cure-all when deeper issues lurk under the surface. Nevertheless, dealing with this issue in your home can be beneficial even if there are other problems besides screen time. It can keep underlying problems from metastasizing, like cancer does.

I'll touch on this subject again in the chapter titled Handle with Care, which provides some counsel on dealing with conflict or potential conflict with your children regarding smartphones.

As you embark on this reading journey, pause for a moment and consider the illustration from the movie Gremlins. You may be in the midst of a monstrous mess because you mistakenly thought that the smartphone would be a reasonable addition to your household, but now the cute idea has morphed into real life problems. Some of them might even be a bit scary to face. Don't lose heart; this is a time for courage. Your children are worth fighting for.

On the other hand, you may be a parent newly embarking on the journey of parenting. Maybe you have an infant or a toddler. This book can be a lifesaver. Setting a good course for your children at the beginning is often easier than correcting a bad course during the teenage years.

In 2011, I produced a documentary called *Captivated: Finding Freedom in a Media Captive Culture*. A portion of the documentary focused on early child development. Many parents across the country and around the world watched the movie and made some needed lifestyle and parenting changes. I met one of these moms at a conference a few years ago who shared with me that she and her husband took to heart the helpful guidance provided by the experts featured in the film and the compelling real-life stories. She said that they also shared the documentary with a group of their friends who were also beginning their parenting journey. This small network of families decided to do things differently than the default cultural current was doing. Years later, they were witnessing the difference in their children compared with other families who didn't have a distinct vision for handling media, entertainment, and technology in their homes.

I hope to hear similar stories from families like yours. Let's band together and save our households from being consumed alive by smartphones.

CHAPTER 2

CAN THE SMARTPHONE BE TAMED?

Here's a big question: can smartphones be tamed? You can test this by taking all the smartphones in your house and putting them in the center of a table and leaving them alone for twenty-four hours. Check on them the next day to see if they've gotten into any trouble. Nothing will have happened.

That wouldn't be the case if you tried the same experiment with a half dozen kittens or just two puppies or one toddler. Bring a wild tiger into your home and let it loose. What do you think is going to happen? In comparison, smartphones are mostly tamed. If you mute the volume, turn off notifications, put it down, and ignore it, it does nothing. Maybe there's a better question; can we be tamed?

I just mentioned that smartphones are mostly tamed. What did I mean by that? There are some problematic elements to the default settings on smartphones. Plus, there's the design and intention of popular apps to hook you and keep you. You may enjoy fishing for recreation, but no one likes to be the one being fished.

Worse yet, being hooked and reeled in. I've written more about this topic in the chapter called Ten Tips for Taming Tech and how you can tame your phone. For now, the priority issue is taming ourselves.

As parents, we are struggling to handle the new technologies without letting them take over our own lives, much less the struggles our kids are facing today. Is it inevitable that we will be under the spell of technology instead of technology being under our control? What does the path ahead look like for our children? What does it look like for us? Let's first try to determine where we are before plotting a path forward.

Is there really a problem or is a book like this just sensationalism? It's a fair question. I've been speaking to youth and parents about the subject of media, entertainment, and technology for over twenty years, and I must confess that for most of that time it has been an uphill struggle. A majority of youth and their parents really weren't interested in the subject of discernment, self-control, and making wise choices. That attitude has begun to change in recent years. Why?

Today, most adults recognize some of the problems they and their children are facing in the digital age. If I say there's a problem today, most parents agree and are hoping to find some solutions. On top of that, there has been a small shift in our culture among some in the tech industry, along with some concerned students, and even some politicians who are becoming alarmed by the latest research on mental and physical health in teens. There are a growing number of organizations focused on awareness, advocacy, and government policy when it comes to screentime and children, especially concerning social media platforms.

Did you know that children, ages eight to ten, spend an average of six hours a day staring at entertainment media on screens? This does not include screentime for school or homework. This research, published by the Center for Disease Control[1], also reported that children, ages eleven to fourteen, spend a whopping nine hours per day on average in front of screens! Teens, aged fifteen to eighteen, spend around seven and a half hours a day watching entertainment media on screens. These new habits are forming the culture of this generation. That's besides the issue of the content of what kids are watching and engaging with on screens or how it impacts their worldview and understanding of morality and faith.

Screen time statistics for adults are not any better. In blog post by Fabio Duarte, he writes, "According to recent data, the average person spends 4 hours and 37 minutes on their phone every day."[2] That's just for smartphone usage and doesn't account for other screen time. A report by Tiago Faia at Techreport.com said, "The average screen time in America is 7 hours and 4 minutes per day."[3] Surprisingly, the U.S. is not the global leader in screen time. In fact, it's not even in the top ten. South Africa, Brazil, and the Philippines hold the top spots.[4]

In 2013, mobile devices accounted for 17 percent of all internet traffic. In 2023, that number had climbed to 60 percent.[5]

According to a report by Trevor Wheelwright, "The average American checks their phone 205 times a day"[6] This habit is now known as checking behavior. A definition given by Microsoft Copilot said, "Checking behavior refers to the habitual and often unconscious act of frequently looking at one's phone for notifications, messages, or updates. This behavior is characterized by the repetitive and sometimes compulsive need to access the device, often driven by the anticipation of new information or social interactions."[7] Another study refers to this smartphone behavior as checking habits.[8]

The Environmental Protection Agency has calculated that a dripping faucet, at the rate of one drip per second, equals three thousand gallons of water in a year if it's not stopped. That's especially shocking when you consider that it takes over fifteen thousand drips to add up to a single gallon of water. If we apply this metaphor to today's use of smartphones, many adults, along with their children, are losing focus, one drip at a time.

Despite the 24/7 connection through social media, teens today are growing more lonely, anxious, and depressed. Why? Because superficial digital connections don't meet the deepest needs of their lives. Many teens are struggling with identity and understanding the purpose and meaning of life. One study has shown that the rise of teenage depression and suicide follows the upward trend of the use of social media.[9] The rise also follows the upward trend of smartphone usage by teens.[10] Even more problematic is the fact that the age of children who have smartphones keeps getting younger, which means they are being exposed to the milieu of issues at earlier ages. Half of all children in the U.S. have a smartphone by the age of eleven.[11]

So, for now, let's get back to the question posed at the beginning of this chapter, "Can the smartphone be tamed?" The answer is yes; the smartphone can be tamed, but the bigger issue is ourselves. A smartphone might be one of the most advanced technologies that everyone carries around with them today, but they are not as complex as humans, and they don't have a soul.

Smartphones are not as complex as personalities, relationships, personal goals, and the pursuit of finding meaning in this life. Smartphones are not as wonderful as the pursuit of God or as needful as healthy family connections or a replacement for deep friendships or the solution to knowing what it means to be loved. Smartphones do not fulfill the deepest needs in our lives, but they are now consuming the majority of a child's free time.

There are endless things for good or for bad that may be discovered on a pocket-sized device that connects to the internet, but at what cost? The most important discoveries in this life happen in the real world, but those discoveries are eroding quickly, and the results are not a better, happier, or more whole childhood.

Before we go any further, I think it may be helpful to give you some encouragement as a parent. First off, there is no such thing as a perfect parent. All parents are flawed to some degree, and though we shouldn't use that fact as an excuse to not take our job seriously, we also need a little grace along the way. Actually, we need a lot of grace along the way.

If you are discouraged with parenting in the digital age, remember that parenting has always been challenging. If you read Genesis, the first book of the Bible, you'll find much disfunction in families. The first family on the planet had to deal with a brother murdering a brother. Whatever you are facing, I hope it's not that dark. God doesn't give up on us, and we shouldn't get discouraged and give up on doing what we can to help our families thrive.

What does it mean to thrive? How you define "thrive" will make a significant difference in how you approach the following pages and whether you find them helpful. Noah Webster's 1828 dictionary says that thrive means "to grow, to advance; to increase or advance in anything valuable."

Just in case you think the Webster's 1828 may be too archaic to help a family in the twenty-first century, let's consider what a Google search uncovers, "grow or develop well or vigorously (of a child, animal, or plant)"

To thrive as a family means you're increasing or advancing in what is valuable according to God. He is the Author of humanity and invented the potential for people, animals, and plants to thrive. Better yet, He has a plan for you and your family to live life to the fullest. How do I know that? Consider these words from Jesus in John 10:10 (GNB), which say, "The thief comes only in order to steal, kill, and destroy. I have come in order that you might have life—life in all its fullness."

So, what does this have to do with media, technology, and children? This modern era has ushered in unprecedented obstacles alongside amazing opportunities when it comes to raising children. The digital age has swept rapidly upon the world, bringing many new blessings and new burdens. These changes have the potential to help your family advance in the right direction or to keep your family from thriving if not handled with care.

The Christian response to these sweeping changes covers a broad spectrum. At one end of the extreme is aversion and disallowance; on the opposite end, you find heedless enthusiasm. In the space between those poles, you can find Christians who are complacent and yield submissive compliance with the strong cultural current. There are better options: deliberate discernment, reasonable convictions, careful handling, purposeful use, and self-control.

> Do you not know that those who run in a race all run, but one receives the prize? Run in such a way that you may obtain it. And everyone who competes for the prize is temperate [exercises self-control] in all things. Now they do it to obtain a perishable crown, but we for an imperishable crown.—1 Corinthians 9:24-25

Thriving is not the ultimate goal; instead, it's a by-product of a healthy family culture that is focused on Jesus. When we talk about culture, we might need to be reminded that the word *culture* has its origin in agriculture. It was about cultivating plants.

What is the culture of your household? Who is influencing it the most? Are you ready to provide good soil and deliberate cultivation in your home in order to grow, to advance; to increase or advance in anything valuable?

As I bring this chapter to a close, remember that I started it with the question, "Can the smartphone be tamed?" Hopefully, I have made the case that we should be asking if we can be tamed. The answer is yes, but not without God's help and not without our willingness to make some brave changes.

ENDNOTES

1. "CDC - Infographics - Screen Time Vs. Lean Time - NCCDPHP: Community Health," n.d. https://archive.cdc.gov/www_cdc_gov/healthyschools/physicalactivity/getmoving.htm.

2. Duarte, Fabio. "Time Spent Using Smartphones (2025 Statistics)." Exploding Topics (blog), June 5, 2025. https://explodingtopics.com/blog/smartphone-usage-stats.

3. Faia, Tiago. "Techreport." Techreport, August 1, 2025. https://techreport.com/statistics/lifestyle/screen-time-statistics/.

4. Faia, "Techreport."

5. Flynn, Jack. "18 Average Screen Time Statistics [2023]: How Much Screen Time Is Too Much?" Zippia, June 29, 2023. https://www.zippia.com/advice/average-screen-time-statistics/.

6. Wheelwright, Trevor. "Cell Phone Usage Stats 2025: Americans Check Their Phones 205 Times a Day." Reviews.org, February 7, 2025. https://www.reviews.org/mobile/cell-phone-addiction/.

7. Microsoft Copilot. "Definition of Checking Behavior." Copilot AI conversation, 2024.

8. Oulasvirta, Antti, Tye Rattenbury, Lingyi Ma, and Eeva Raita. "Habits Make Smartphone Use More Pervasive." Personal and Ubiquitous Computing 16, no. 1 (June 15, 2011): 105–14. https://doi.org/10.1007/s00779-011-0412-2.

9. Vidal, C., Lhaksampa, T., Miller, L., & Platt, R. (2020). Social media use and depression in adolescents: a scoping review. International Review of Psychiatry, 32(3), 235–253. https://doi.org/10.1080/09540261.2020.1720623

10. Samuel Hunley PhD and Samuel Hunley PhD, "Does Smartphone Use Effect Your Anxiety and Depression?," Anxiety Disorders and Universal Health Care, March 4, 2024, https://web.archive.org/web/20240917083156/https://www.anxiety.org/smartphone-use-and-its-relationship-to-anxiety-and-depression.

11. Anya Kamenetz, "Report: More Than Half of U.S. Children Now Own a Smartphone by Age 11," NPR, October 29, 2019, https://www.npr.org/2019/10/29/774306250/report-more-than-half-of-u-s-children-now-own-a-smartphone-by-age-11.

CHAPTER 3

HEALTH FOOD AND GOAT YOGA

I never thought I'd entertain the idea of alien abductions. I don't believe that creatures from outer space come down to Earth in flying saucers and kidnap humans for experiments. On the other hand, there's something strange happening to families today when screens in the average household outnumber the people, and everyone is fixated on their devices. The seemingly ubiquitous behavior in most homes makes me wonder what's going on.

Have you been wondering if strange creatures from another world have abducted your kids and swapped them for some look-alikes who are lacking the heart and soul of your family? You probably want your family back, right? You're under the same roof, but everyone seems to live on their own planet.

Parents are often quick to become frustrated with children and teens when they are glued to the smartphone and continually distracted. How would we have handled the powerful lure of smartphones when we were teens if we had access to the world's largest collection of music, video games, movies, pornography, and 24/7 connections to our peers, all in the palm of our hand? In addition to being sponsored by Mom and Dad? I honestly don't think we would have fared better, but that doesn't mean our children don't need a course correction.

As we delve into this subject of smartphones and other disrupting technologies it's helpful to have a goal in mind. What do you hope will change? What do you want to recover that seems to be lost? What is broken and needs to be fixed? Let's think about some possible goals.

Are you tempted to move your family to Alaska and live off the grid without technology? Or are you secretly yearning for Little House on the Prairie? Maybe your goal is something a bit more simplistic: you just want tech-savvy children who don't act like zombies! Hopefully, you are seeking to find balance and regain focus in your home. A balanced food diet can be a helpful analogy. One of the more prominent goals of our culture today is physical health and wellness. This goal motivates people to eat healthy foods and get more and exercise.

We live in a culture that is becoming increasingly more conscious regarding diet and exercise. Organic, non-GMO, and locally sourced foods are in vogue. Many grocery stores today have gluten free sections, alternatively sweetened treats, and grain free snacks. You can choose to go on a paleo diet or a Mediterranean diet or do intermittent fasting or even try a carnivore diet.

Vitamins, supplements, essential oils, and superfoods promise to do wonders. Then there's our microbiome health that can be helped through kombucha, kefir, kimchi, yogurt, and other fermented foods.

Add to the mix the exercise craze with CrossFit, tai chi, health club memberships, water workouts, wellness coaches, planking, parkour, exercise apps, Fitbits, and—goat yoga? It's all supposed to give us better health, more happiness, and a longer life.

The reason behind this fixation on exercise and healthy eating is because we understand that our bodies are affected by the food we eat and whether or not we get regular exercise. A junk food diet is going to have a negative effect on your body in the long term if that's all you eat. And if you don't get any exercise, you will likely be less healthy.

But what does your family's media diet look like? Are you eager to make wise and healthy choices about entertainment and tech use? What's on your digital plate? I like to describe our present culture as an all-you-can-eat media and entertainment buffet, and we pile a lot of content onto our plates! Have you thought about how your daily media diet affects your spiritual health? Family health? Physical health? Emotional health? Mental health?

There are three main concerns when it comes to the all-you-can-eat media buffet that we experience every day. The first is the amount of media and entertainment on your plates each day, week, and year. The amount or quantity of screen time you watch is what I refer to as your media consumption. I find it interesting that a food consumption metaphor has become fully integrated into new media habits when referencing the act of "binging" on episodic shows on streaming platforms. The well-known Christian leader, George Barna, once wrote, "Media exposure has become America's most widespread and serious addiction."

The second concern you need to consider is the quality of the media on your plate. Is it healthy, or like junk food, or possibly even toxic? The quality of your screen time is what I refer to as media content.

When I first began speaking and writing about media discernment, my primary focus was about guarding the heart and mind from compromising content. That concern has not gone away, but there's been an exponential shift in the last decade with the growing problem of media consumption—not just the content but also how much media we are absorbed with. Much of that consumption has to do with the convenient access through devices that fit in our pockets.

The third concern is with the technologies, especially the smartphone, that are used to access all this content. With the increasingly high rates of screen time around the globe, I've often wondered if it is possible for people to reach a media saturation threshold? Is there a point when all your waking hours are spent interacting with a screen? At the same time, you recognize there is still something missing in your life, but you have no time for reflection to find out what it is.

As you consider your goals, I want to point you to an essential starting point. How about starting with restored and healthy relationships? How about a healthy relationship between you and your children? That sounds like a good goal. How about healthy friendships for your children? That also sounds like a winner. How about a restored relationship with the Creator of the universe through faith in Jesus Christ?

There are important secondary goals that will help your family with setting a balanced and healthy trajectory in this digital age. We are going to learn about those in other chapters, but I wouldn't be doing you any favors to talk about those things and neglect to remind you of the greatest priority in life—to follow Jesus.

You may be wondering how following Jesus will help us as parents if we are struggling with tech in the home? The parenting challenges we are facing are not merely tech problems but also heart problems, worldview problems, and outside and outsized influencer problems. Our call to follow Jesus is at the crossroads of all these real-life issues, and they matter to Him as much as they matter to us.

No doubt, misuse, overuse, or compulsive use of today's media, entertainment, and technologies have become some of the greatest obstacles for spiritual growth and family health. It can be easy to think that the goal is to get technology and media under control, and then you're all good to go. But if your main goal is anything other than following Jesus and helping your children also to follow Him, then your goals in life are shortsighted and do not have the best interest of your children in mind.

SHOULD PHONE RADIATION BE A CONCERN?

Some believe there is cause for concern about the negative effects of radiation from your phone, and others dismiss it as a non-issue. Even though the possible negative effects are debatable, the fact that your phone gives off radiation is not debatable. Phone manufacturers are required to publish the amount of radiation for each model they produce. It's also not debatable that the waves emitted from cellphone towers are also a form of radiation.

I'm not bringing up the subject of radiation to stoke conspiracy theories or to deny the possibility that a day may come when the debate no longer exists and the harm of having a high-powered receiver in our pockets becomes known as a bad idea that should have been thought through more carefully.

I mention this issue because there are reasonable steps that we can take that do not keep us from using smartphones but may prove to be wise decisions in how we use them. I personally don't keep my phone in my pocket throughout the day. It may be uncool, but I keep mine in a holster on my belt, and I've worn it this way for years. I truly don't know whether this method is better or not when it comes to radiation, but the reason I bring it up is that it certainly doesn't hurt my use of a phone, even if in the end it doesn't help.

I also try not to have long conversations on my phone with the device up against my ear. I've previously used wireless earpieces (which are also controversial to some). However, my default for many years has been to use a small pair of wired earbuds for long conversations or I just put my phone on speaker mode if the environment is conducive and keep the phone away from my head. I know the concern about possible negative effects from phone radiation may sound uncool and unnecessary, maybe both are true, but I'm just sharing an example of what some people may choose to do out of caution. This issue isn't the biggest one I want to address in the book, but it does play a part in our journey forward.

Like today's health and wellness crazes that require goals and discipline, the negative effects of today's media and technology warrant our attention and the same zeal for protecting our children and helping them to thrive in the digital age.

CHAPTER 4

NEITHER TECHNOPHOBE NOR TECHNOPHILE

Let me give you a little background about myself. I've been speaking to youth and parents about media, entertainment, and technology for over two decades. This predates smartphones, YouTube, Netflix, Facebook, X (formerly Twitter), Instagram, Snapchat, TikToxic, and more. I'm also a dad who has helped my wife raise our four children. Our youngest is now eighteen years old.

Another important disclaimer is that I'm not anti-media, anti-technology, or even anti-entertainment. But any parent today would be in denial to not admit that things are out of balance, and we are losing focus. In his book, Technopoly, Neil Postman writes,

> It is a mistake to suppose that any technological innovation has a one-sided effect. Every technology is both a burden and a blessing; not either-or, but this-and-that.

We are currently surrounded by throngs of…one eye-eyed prophets who see only what new technologies can do and incapable of imagining what they will undo. We might call such people Technophiles. They gaze on technology as a love does on his beloved, seeing it as without blemish and entertaining no apprehension for the future…The Technophiles must speak for themselves, and do so all over the place. My defense is that a dissenting voice is sometimes needed to moderate the din made by the enthusiastic multitudes.

Postman published these words over thirty years ago!

Could you imagine going two weeks without screens? No smartphone, no internet, no social media, no texts, no movies, or TV shows? Probably not, and neither could I when I was a teen.

It is common for teens to think *but it doesn't affect me!* when defending their consumption of media. I sincerely believed that my media choices didn't influence me, but then something happened that radically changed my perspective. At the age of seventeen, I became serious about following Jesus Christ. I attended a special youth event, and the speaker talked about being sold out for Jesus and living a surrendered life to Him.

As far as I remember, I don't think entertainment was mentioned specifically, but the Holy Spirit began to convict my heart about my media choices: the music I listened to, the movies I watched, the amount of time spent playing video games, and sitting in front of the TV every week to catch my favorite shows. I would say that my personal habits were not extreme in comparison to my peers. I was average, but being average didn't mean my habits weren't a problem.

At the time, I didn't realize that God was speaking to my heart about these things; I just thought I was having a debate with myself. Do you know what I was saying inside? If you guessed, "But it doesn't affect me," then you are right. That was exactly what I was saying in defense of myself. Then, God went a little deeper into my heart and asked me if I was willing to lay these things aside? Do you know my response? *But it doesn't affect me, so it's not an issue.* Then, in my heart, I realized something that disturbed me about myself: my answer was no. I would not give these things up if God asked me to.

I couldn't shake these gnawing thoughts, and I was troubled by how defensive I was. Suddenly, I realized for the first time that electronic media really had a hold on my life. I didn't understand how or why, but it was apparent that regulating my media choices was something I struggled with.

Though I didn't yet believe that my media choices were affecting me negatively, I knew saying no to God would be wrong if there was something He wanted me to do. My initial unwillingness to let go hardly lined up with what it meant to be a disciple of Jesus. I decided I would give up electronic media for two weeks. No radio, no cassette tapes, no Nintendo, no TV, no movies. Of course, there was no smartphone, internet, social media, iTunes, or Netflix only because they didn't exist in the late 80's. I only knew one person in my graduating class who had the internet at home but that was because his father worked for the U.S. military, and honestly, I really didn't understand what the internet was after my friend tried to explain it.

So, was it hard for me to do go on this media fast? Yes, it was, initially. But guess what happened? I began to experience a new-found freedom in my life that I didn't know was missing before. I began to see God more clearly, and a needed detox was happening in my heart and mind.

Jesus said, "Blessed are the pure in heart for they shall see God." I compare it to the difference between looking up at the sky at night in a big city like Chicago and you can't see the stars because of all the light pollution. But if you get out to the country, beyond all the manmade lights and look up, you can see the stars, the constellations, and the band of the Milky Way galaxy. It's amazing.

All the potential quiet space in my life was filled with noise and the visual and emotional stimulation of screens, but I didn't realize how much they clouded my vision until I made it all go away for those two weeks.

Now, before you get nervous and start thinking, "I'm going to bail on this book if he's going to say that we've got to get rid of all our media," you're jumping to the wrong conclusion. Please hear me out. This two-week reset was really helpful, and it did lead to some long-term changes in my life, but I haven't lived my life since then with no media or entertainment or without utilizing modern technologies. I like watching good movies, I love listening to music, and my smartphone is a helpful multipurpose tool, but before I could establish some balance in my life, it was beneficial to take that media fast.

I'm a fan of going on a media fast but it's not a permanent solution. In this book I want to help you establish a healthy media diet. You may want to consider some intermittent media fasting, even if it means carving out some time each day for some undistracted time in your life. A break from screens now and then would be helpful to you.

One helpful action step is to consider a media fast of some sort, maybe for part of a day, or an entire day, or if you are adventurous you might try for a week or two like I did as a teen.

Once again, fasting from media is not the end goal; it's simply a helpful tool that can help you gain some quiet in your life and allow you to reevaluate the amount of media and entertainment you are consuming. Being enthusiastic about a media fast is much more challenging if you're unsure whether the effort will make any difference in your life. You may not know the answer until you try. My break from media certainly made a difference in my life.

CHAPTER 5

THE GREAT DIGITAL MIGRATION

In 2001, a man named Marc Prensky was credited for coining the terms digital natives and digital immigrants. The purpose of the terminology was to make a distinction between two groups of people based on what they thought and how they interacted with the revolutionary tools and toys of the digital age.

Are you a digital native or a digital immigrant? If you are young parent, you are likely a digital native, or if you are a little older and have teens, your teens are certainly digital natives.

I am considered a digital immigrant. Digital natives began to emerge with children who were born during the 1980's or later, who grew up with a personal computer, the internet, video games, and more. These were not new technologies to them because they always existed in their lives. Because of their exposure to these new devices from a young age, they easily adapted to the new technologies that came wave after wave upon the shores of our new digital society.

Digital immigrants, like me, remember a world without computers, the internet, digital music, video games, cellphones, or even cordless phones, for that matter. We thought it was cool when the landline wasn't attached to the wall by a cord anymore.

I remember when my parents brought home a Commodore 64 that predated the Atari 2600 in our household for playing video games. I remember when they upgraded our stereo system and debated whether they should buy the latest breakthrough in digital audio, a Compact Disc player. They didn't; they bought a new record player instead.

We didn't have a personal computer in our home the entire time I was in school, the closest thing was an electric typewriter, and that is hardly close. The most amazing new tech when I was a teen was the invention of the Sony Walkman, the small personal cassette player with headphones. They were all the rage after the fading trend of the boombox (I had one of those also).

However, my children who were born in the late nineties into the 2000's have always known home computers, MP3's, the internet, Amazon, cellphones, and other wireless technologies. They are natives. What is difficult for immigrants and natives to understand is that we don't always think the same way about these technologies.

If your children are twelve years or older, they've experienced most of the latest changes including VR, augmented reality, Snapchat, Instagram, Pinterest, TikTok, Twitch, Netflix, iTunes, Facetime, and video conferencing, such as Zoom.

Some of you may be too young to know that the modern smart phone is like a crossbreed of a PDA, an iPod, and a cellphone. The PDA might be making you scratch your head. I'm not talking about the acronym for Public Display of Affection. PDAs were personal digital assistants, a business tool to keep a calendar, take notes, set alarms, and such, but it wasn't a phone and didn't play music or videos. One of the predecessors to the modern smartphone was the BlackBerry used by business professionals and sometimes referred to as a "CrackBerry" because of its addictive nature. It was a harbinger for what was coming and should have been a warning for all of us. Apple changed the world we know when it introduced the iPhone in 2007.

So much has changed in the last twenty years and is changing still. These technological advances are exciting no doubt, but with all the enthusiasm, there is need for pause and reflection. What will we allow ourselves to become if we don't think deeply about the way our technologies are changing us as people, as families, as communities? The answer to that question is why I am writing this book and why I started a nonprofit organization in 2005 to help families learn how to handle media and technology with care. I want to help you think deeply about these issues so that you can thrive spiritually, physically, emotionally, and socially in this new era. We are living in a unique time in world history, and it calls for new skills in parenting. It can be a precarious learning curve because our own parents didn't face these new challenges.

NO ANCESTRAL WISDOM

For example, if I went to my parents to ask for advice about parenting and smartphones, they would have no experience as parents with this issue. They have no ancestral wisdom to share, no helpful hints passed down from generation to generation. Parents today are blazing new trails for better or for worse. So here we are, wandering through the techno jungle without a clear path ahead and ignorant of the dangers and pitfalls before us.

My dad recalls watching television as a young child from the wash tub on the kitchen floor being used for his weekly bath.

The TV was a new addition to the house, and it predated a flushing toilet in the family. They were still using an outhouse at the time. Smartphones were nonexistent during his childhood and throughout most of his adult life, including his years raising my brothers and me.

Not only is there no ancestral wisdom, but also it seems that there is no real cultural wisdom that has clearly emerged to help parents today choose a good course for their children and themselves concerning the smartphone and modern technology. This is where I endeavor to help through this book and pass along what bits and pieces of ponderings and experiences I have gleaned from a few thoughtful trailblazers. I'm not only passing along thoughts from others, but also my own ideas I've gathered in my search for wisdom for over thirty years.

We can't go back to the way things were before the smartphone even if we wanted to. The path ahead must be to train ourselves and our children to use technology with wisdom and not let it control our lives.

Let's hope that in the near future, parents like you will not only help their own children learn how to handle technology with wisdom but also prepare them to share what they've learned with the next generation. Let's begin building ancestral wisdom together, starting now.

CHAPTER 6

WHY DO WE GIVE OUR CHILDREN SMARTPHONES?

Over the years, as I have interacted with parents, I've yet to experience a conversation where the parents tell me how wonderful life has become now that they've given their child a smartphone. I'm not saying it hasn't happened; I'm just saying I haven't encountered this scenario. Most conversations about the subject are about parents asking for help because the smartphone has morphed into a devious little monster. Or more accurately, their children have changed because of smartphones.

Someone once coined the catchy phrase, "If you always do what you always did, you will always get what you always got." The quote has been attributed to Henry Ford, Albert Einstein, and Mark Twain. We might have lingering doubts about the origin of the quote, but a more important question to ask is why are parents giving smartphones to their children? A variety of reasons can be found. For one, it's an electronic babysitter on steroids, a convenient pacifier that can satisfy short term goals.

Just look around you whenever you are in public and start counting how many toddlers you see holding a phone or a tablet and watching or interacting with the screen as Mom or Dad pushes them around in a stroller. You find the same behavior happening with toddlers while families eat out at restaurants. Just the other day I witnessed a teenage girl at an adjacent table while I was taking my wife and daughter out to lunch. The girl was with her dad and mom, wearing noise cancelling headphones, and I could see that she was watching a movie on her phone the entire time they were there. The behavior clearly doesn't always stop when toddlers grow up.

Another reason parents give their children smartphones is the growing cultural expectations. Other adults may think you are neglecting your child and even harming them if you don't give them a smartphone. But what if the opposite was actually happening? What if you are harming or hindering your children's wellbeing by giving them a phone? I'm getting ahead of myself, but a compelling case can be made that you are not doing your children any favors when you prematurely give them a phone.

Then, there's peer pressure for children to have a smartphone like all their friends do. Other times, the parents are over-enthusiastic about technology. For others, it can be a decision based on unwarranted fears that their child will not be able to keep up with the times. You may be afraid your children will be educationally and socially stymied if they don't have a smartphone or will be technologically behind the times and never be able to catch up in the rapidly changing world.

One of the biggest dupes comes from the false idea that a child or a teen has an unalienable right to a phone. Teens have wrongly reimagined the Declaration of Independence as promising life, liberty, and having a smartphone. Having a phone is not a right;

it's a privilege that requires a tremendous amount of responsibility. There are certain stages of a child's development when they are not ready for the responsibility and, therefore, shouldn't have the privilege. Even when a child is at an appropriate age to handle bigger responsibilities, privileges can be and should be withheld or revoked when they fail to show responsibility.

Did I miss anything when it comes to the question of why we give children phones? Oh yes, to keep track of them through GPS capabilities, to stay connected with them when they are away from home, or to be able to reach each other in case of an emergency. These reasons can be legitimate ones, while many of the former ones I have mentioned are founded on thin, weak arguments.

What do you fear your children will be missing out on if you delay giving them a smartphone? Are you fearful that they will be out of step with culture? Do you think they will be socially backward? Are you afraid that they will not become technologically savvy in this digital revolution? Are you fearful that they will be bored? Have no friends? Be ostracized?

Have you thought about what you will be denying them by giving them a smartphone? Have you thought about how much weight is being loaded on them, which they will have to carry through their childhood into the tumultuous season of adolescence? That load gets even heavier as they navigate their middle school and high school years.

Have you considered how the smartphone can shut down creative play and stunt a child's imagination? How many children today are missing out on cultivating in-person friendships because of the smartphone? Are you aware of how it has disrupted physical exercise and outdoor activities? Have you carefully researched the documented problems of anxiety and depression stemming from social media, online bullying, online predators, sexting, pornography, sleep deprivation, and an agitated nervous system that has become part and parcel with today's smartphone usage among children and teens?

Going back to the subject of education, did you know that studies have shown that giving kids laptops or tablets to use in the classroom and for homework has not resulted in better academic outcomes? I interviewed professor and author Mark Bauerlein in my documentary *Captivated: Finding Freedom in a Media Captive Culture* who wrote an informative book called *The Dumbest Generation: How the Digital Age Stupefies Young Americans and Jeopardizes Our Future*. The following is an excerpt from the publisher about the book.

> We assumed that teens would use their knowledge and understanding of technology to set themselves apart as the vanguards of this new digital era. That was the promise. But the enlightenment didn't happen. The technology that was supposed to make young adults more aware, diversify their tastes, and improve their verbal skills has had the opposite effect. According to recent reports from the National Endowment for the Arts, most young people in the United States do not read literature, visit museums, or vote. They cannot explain basic scientific methods, recount basic American history, name their local political representatives, or locate Iraq or Israel on a map.

Jonathan Haidt in his book *The Anxious Generation* advocates for phones to be banned in all schools. He's not joking! And this proposed action step is based on research data. The nonprofit organization *Fairplay* has the following statement on their website:

Fairplay has partnered with the Phone-Free Schools Movement (PFSM), an organization dedicated to helping K-12 students excel academically and socially by eliminating the harms caused by phones in schools. Cell phones are a major distraction for students. Depression and anxiety rates have skyrocketed, and over 40 percent of students who use social media the most say their mental health is poor or very poor. On the flip side, students not using their phones during class wrote down 62 percent more information, and 83 percent of teachers say they support an all-day phone-free school policy. By working with PSFM, we at Fairplay are responding to the growing call from teachers, school leaders, parents and kids themselves to get phones out of the school environment.[1]

Besides the direct, negative impact on children having smartphones, have you considered the sacrifice required of all the good things they could be doing with that time lost in the black hole of screentime? We are not talking about a few minutes out of each day but several hours every day! Hours that may have been spent doing something beneficial.

Marshall McLuhan, who is known as the father of media literacy, in his well-known book *Understanding Media: The Extensions of Man* (1975), demonstrated how modern technologies are often invented to extend ourselves.

Take for instance the invention or technology of the bicycle. It extends our legs. We can go farther, faster with wheels and pedals underneath us. We can function without a bicycle and walk from point A to point B, but a bicycle extends our legs and makes us faster. This example is a simple illustration of using technology to extend ourselves. McLuhan applied this concept to media technologies. He may not have imagined the smartphone, but he did predict the World Wide Web thirty years before it was invented.

In his book, he also used the metaphor of amputations. We may be in awe of the extensions yet not be aware of the potential amputations that may also be taking place because of the new technologies. By amputations, he meant something that is lost in the process of embracing the new technologies.

We are all learning through experience about the "extensions of man" through our daily use of smartphones. In many ways, a smartphone is a digital Swiss army knife with an unbelievable variety of tools conveniently held in your pocket.

Do you know that there are amputations already happening in our children and in our homes because of this technology? Some are easy to spot, and others may be more subtle but equally damaging. Consider the loss of quiet and reflection.

Do you believe quiet and reflection is needful in life? I hope so. Do you realize that they are quickly eroding away in our lives, and our children may not even know what is happening. Our children don't know what they are missing and don't know that experiencing quiet is important and worth pursuing in life. The loss of quiet reflection is an example of something being amputated as we have overextended ourselves. Before smartphones and other portable technologies, there were unavoidable moments every day for quiet and reflection when we were alone. When in the presence of other people, there was an opportunity for conversation, which is something else eroding today. But how can someone, especially a teen, intentionally shift if they don't know what it is they are missing? How can they take aim when they don't know what the target is?

I believe there is something intrinsic, something instinctive in humanity that beckons us to pause and experience quiet in our lives, yet every waking moment is now inundated with digital distractions or diversions as soon as these potential moments for quiet arise. Unfortunately, this instinct can be easily drowned out through our constant access to the internet on our phones. Our modern default has trained us to be uneasy with quiet and reflection. We have been programmed to pick up the phone and open to our home screen as soon as the slightest blank space appears in our lives.

For those of us who are digital immigrants, we can hopefully still remember the times when there was nothing else to do but daydream, contemplate our surroundings, reflect on the day, compose something in our head, or simply experience a moment of wonder. The loss of quiet is like having a good friend who has been locked up in a prison unjustly and then forgotten. Instead, we have a new acquaintance in our lives who is loud, boisterous, and never stops seeking our attention.

Most of the books being written on this subject come from a humanistic, naturalistic, and evolutionary worldview. With that framework, these authors acknowledge that we are currently overwhelmed in ways that are not natural to us and are seemingly beyond our ability to process. They believe that our brains have not evolved as fast as the modern technologies. They think there is some catching up to do before our brains can handle the firehose of information and the seemingly infinite trails of diversion now accessible to everyone. I don't believe in the theory of evolution. We were created by God, and He designed us with a tremendous amount of adaptability. But I don't believe we will adapt to the point of eradicating the need for quiet in our lives for our own good and for our relationship with God.

The Bible says in Psalms 46:10, "Be still, and know that I am God; I will be exalted among the nations, I will be exalted in the earth!" Psalms 4:4 tells us, "Meditate within your heart on your bed, and be still." Psalms 77:12 states, "I will also meditate on all Your work, and talk of Your deeds," And Psalms 143:5 says, "I remember the days of old; I meditate on all Your works; I muse on the work of Your hands."

The New Testament also reminds us of the need to think deeply about certain things. Philippians 4:8 says, "Finally, brethren, whatever things are true, whatever things are noble, whatever things are just, whatever things are pure, whatever things are lovely, whatever things are of good report, if there is any virtue and if there is anything praiseworthy—meditate on these things."

When writing the draft of this chapter, I was on a layover in a busy airport. I sat in a particularly busy hub with a second-floor balcony furnished with rocking chairs. Below, a pianist played popular tunes on a grand piano. As I penned the words about the need for quiet and reflection, the pianist started playing the hymn *Be Still My Soul*. I don't know how you would have reacted, but I stopped writing and simply soaked in that beautiful moment with a sense of wonder. It gives me chills even now just remembering it. The song was written in 1752 by Kathrina von Schlegel and translated in 1855 by Jane Borthwick. The hymn is a wonderful reminder of our fleeting time on Earth and the eternal joys that await.

> Be still, my soul! The Lord is on thy side;
> Bear patiently the cross of grief or pain.
> Leave to thy God to order and provide;
> In every change He faithful will remain.
> Be still, my soul! Thy best, thy heav'nly Friend
> through thorny ways leads to a joyful end.
>
> Be still, my soul! Thy God doth undertake
> to guide the future as He has the past.

> Thy hope, thy confidence let nothing shake;
> All now mysterious shall be bright at last.
> Be still, my soul! The waves and winds still know
> His voice who ruled them while He dwelt below.
>
> Be still, my soul! When dearest friends depart
> and all is darkened in the veil of tears.
> Then shalt thou better know His love, His heart;
> Who comes to soothe thy sorrow and thy fears.
> Be still, my soul!; Thy Jesus can repay
> from His own fullness all He takes away.
>
> Be still, my soul! The hour is hast'ning on
> when we shall be forever with the Lord,
> when disappointment, grief, and fear are gone,
> sorrow forgot, love's purest joys restored.
> Be still, my soul! When change and tears are past,
> all safe and blessed we shall meet at last.

We probably need song writers today to write us a couple new verses about being still in the technological age.

I began with the question, "Why do we give our children smartphones?" Now I want to ask a more important question, should we give them smartphones? And if so, when? Those questions will be the subject of the next chapter.

ENDNOTES

1. Fairplay, "Fairplay, Phone-Free Schools Movement Announce Partnership, Tools to Help Remove Phones in Schools," Fairplay, July 17, 2024, https://fairplayforkids.org/fairplay-phone-free-schools-movement-announce-partnership-tools-to-help-remove-phones-in-schools/.

CHAPTER 7

DRIVER'S ED

What if your eight-year-old asked you for the keys of your car so that he or she could take it for a drive? I think you would put your foot down. There are good reasons why all fifty states in the U.S. require a written test, supervised practice, and a driving test, not to mention age limits for drivers.

There's also a reason car insurance is high for young people. There's a reason there are driver's education courses with lessons, tests, driving instructions, and more. The example of driver's ed inspired me to adopt the approach I have taken in my home regarding smartphones and the internet. This is what I will be sharing with you in this chapter.

The blueprint for parenting in the digital age that I'm providing in this chapter is not intended as a prescription that you must follow but rather a plan of action for you to consider. It is meant to be a helpful example for you because we don't have ancestral wisdom on this subject!

Before the invention of the automobile, children didn't need driver's ed courses; instead, they needed to learn how to handle horses, buggies, carts, and mules. No doubt, there were dangers and challenges to handling large animals and carts or wagons. But those modes of transportation from the past cannot compare to a modern vehicle weighing over three thousand pounds and moving at speeds often exceeding sixty-five miles per hour. Today, all young aspiring drivers need training and testing. Along the same line, it's time to wake up to the growing need in the 21st century for training and testing before getting a smartphone.

The heedless enthusiasm in our culture for all things tech has resulted in a high rate of moral and spiritual fender benders or, sometimes, something worse. Parents have often asked me for advice about smartphones after their children have experienced the devastation of a crash from getting on pornographic websites and becoming hooked or becoming obsessed with social media to the detriment of their mental and spiritual wellbeing. A growing number of experts agree there's a need for a better parenting model when it comes to smartphones, so I'm going to present a plan for you to consider.

An eight-year-old child in my household didn't have a license to drive on the information superhighway or have a smartphone at his disposal. Like driving a car, there would come a day when I would want my child to learn to drive responsibly, just as I want him to be able to handle a smartphone and the internet. The goal wasn't to keep him from driving a car for the rest of his life, but to start the process at an appropriate age. The same is true for smartphones and access to the internet. My approach was similar to the steps needed for getting a driver's license.

I wanted to train my teens to be collision-free drivers when it comes to cars and have the same seriousness when handling smartphones. I want them to be careful and wise.

I want to make a comparison to the four stages a child goes through to get a driver's license and apply these stages to the steps teens should take to demonstrate they can handle a smartphone with wisdom. What I'm about to share may seem counter-cultural, but it is reasonable.

Here's a quick overview, and then we can dig a little deeper. The first stage is a child's environment. The second stage is about being an intentional mentor to your child. The third stage is the learner's permit with supervised use. The last phase is the driver's test to acquire the privilege of a license.

STAGE 1: ENVIRONMENT

Using the driving analogy, a child grows up as a passenger in a car. Dad or Mom is usually the one in the driver's seat. In the beginning, a baby is secured by an infant seat but gradually moves into a toddler seat and eventually to a booster seat. It's a big deal when graduating to just a seat belt. During these years, a child encounters a driving environment without a conscious awareness of being a driver herself someday.

Let's shift from the analogy to the application. When our kids are young, Dad and Mom set the stage. The child is a passive observer in their early years, but what are they observing? Do they see Mommy and Daddy staring and interacting all the time with a small device that lights up, makes sounds, and keeps their attention? They are not yet active participants, but they are active learners. They are soaking everything in, and their understanding of the world is forming before they can put words together.

This age is not a suitable time in your children's development for them to start watching anything on a screen. To see a toddler pick up a phone and already know how to swipe may seem cute, but cute doesn't mean healthy. Before smartphones, there were many studies that gave insight about young children and television viewing. In 1999, the American Academy of Pediatrics published a recommendation that discouraged parents from television viewing by children under two-years-old. That recommendation was reiterated in 2011.[1] Let me quote from the introduction to this policy statement.

> The AAP believed that there were significantly more potential negative effects of media than positive ones for this age group and, thus, advised families to thoughtfully consider media use for infants. This policy statement reaffirms the 1999 statement with respect to media use in infants and children younger than 2 years and provides updated research findings to support it. This statement addresses (1) the lack of evidence supporting educational or developmental benefits for media use by children younger than 2 years, (2) the potential adverse health and developmental effects of media use by children younger than 2 years, and (3) Adverse effects of parental media use (background media) on children younger than 2 years.

More than a decade later, the AAP still recommends no screen time for children under two except for video calls with family. From two to age five, they recommend no more than an hour a day of quality educational content watched with a parent. The World Health Organization agrees with the limit to one hour of screen time for this age group but also reiterates that less is better.

So, why all the fuss? I interviewed Dr. Dimitri Christakis for my documentary *Captivated* and when asked about the concerns he said, "The newborn's brain triples in size in the first two years of life. It's an extraordinary period of brain growth, unparalleled over the entire life span. And it does that in direct response to external stimulation."

Christakis and other doctors agree that children in the first two years need real life interaction, not glowing screens. It may surprise you that even though an incredibly young child will stay mesmerized by entertainment on a screen, it actually shortens their attention span. Dr. Christakis gave some insight to his research,

> We found that the more television children watch before the age of three, the shorter their attention spans were later. We also found that the more cognitive stimulation that they got before the age of three, and we measured cognitive stimulation by how often you read to your child, how often you take your child to the museum, how often you sing to your child, the kinds of things that many parents think of as being good for babies. We found that the more of those kinds of activities babies had, actually, the less likely they were to have shorter attention spans later in life. So, if you think of it, these are really two sides of the same coin. There are certain things we can do early in a baby's life that promote their attention span, and there are certain things we can do early on that hinder it.

Dr. David Walsh, in my documentary, explained the difference between reactive attention and focused attention.

There are different attention systems within the brain. We have one attention system deep within the brain, in the limbic brain, I call it the reactive attention system. It is involuntary, hardwired, we don't have to learn it. We are hardwired to pay attention to things that move and things that are emotionally stimulating. So, that's the one that's working when I'm deeply engrossed in a great mystery, and out of the very corner of my eye I see a little mouse run along the floorboard. Where would my attention be focused? On that mouse. It's called the orientation response. We're wired to pay attention to things that move or things that are emotionally stimulating. There's another type of attention, that's the one that we use when we are paying attention to something that isn't moving, something that isn't emotionally stimulating. For many kids today who have a very, very heavy media diet, what they have is an overdeveloped reactive attention system and an underdeveloped focused attention system. And so, we have a growing epidemic of distraction because kids are always responding to all of this technology that is constantly vying for their attention. And a lot of the ways that we used to develop the focused attention system have disappeared.

I had an enlightening conversation with Dr. Christakis off camera, and he asked me if I knew what age children began watching TV on average in the U.S. I didn't know. His answer was four months old. Then he asked me if I knew why it was not earlier. Again, I didn't know. He explained it was because at four months, most babies can begin to sit up on their own, which means a parent can plop them in front of a TV, and they'll stare at it. But if we consider what Dr. Walsh said about attention, that baby is not developing any focused attention by staring at a TV. In fact, it is undermining the development for focused attention.

We can't give babies a hard time about their fixation on screens because it's not their fault. It's not my fault either when I'm out to dinner with my wife, and there is a TV on the wall within eyesight. It doesn't matter what's on the TV, it could even be something I couldn't care less about, yet my attention will go to the screen reactively. The captivating lure is frustrating for sure.

Let's consider a few more insights about a child's early environment today. Besides the shorter attention spans, studies have also shown that screen time hinders a child's language learning and cognitive development. According to the American Academy of Pediatrics, "Children younger than 2 years need hands-on exploration and social interaction with trusted caregivers to develop their cognitive, language, motor, and social-emotional skills. Because of their immature symbolic, memory, and attentional skills, infants and toddlers cannot learn from traditional digital media as they do from interactions with caregivers, and they have difficulty transferring that knowledge to their 3-dimensional experience."[2]

Joanna Parga-Belinkie, MD, IBCLC, FAAP, on the website, healthychildren.org writes, "The development of speech and language skills is strongly linked to thinking ability, social relationships, reading, writing, and school success. This development happens when parents and children regularly talk and communicate both with words and without words (verbal and nonverbal interactions). Nothing can take the place of these interactions when it comes to our children's learning and speech and language development. That's why it is important to focus on quality, real-life face time."

As children get older and are exposed to even more screen time, they often neglect needed physical activity, eat more snacks that are less nutritious, and get less sleep than their minds and bodies need. I have an entire chapter in this book devoted to the subject of sleep. The unnatural sedentary behavior of children fixated on screens has sometimes led to problems with childhood obesity. Another notable problem is the delay in children developing needed social skills.

There was a time when homeschooled children were often a target of groundless ridicule for not being properly socialized, but now we know that one of the real problems hindering the development of social skills in children is excessive screen time not home education.

Dr. Victoria Dunckley, in her book *Reset Your Child's Brain: A Four-Week Plan to End Meltdowns, Raise Grades, and Boost Social Skills by Reversing the Effects of Electronic Screen-Time* offers parents practical help for addressing certain problematic behavioral issues by getting kids off screens and engaging them with beneficial activities. She demonstrates that her plan is not merely theoretical but proven to make a difference.

Let's remember why we are thinking about this subject. We are considering a child's environment that they grow up in, and the analogy is a child who is along for the ride in a car being driven by Mom or Dad. One day, when your children come to the appropriate age, you will want them to be able to drive safely and responsibly. But in their younger years, they are mere observers of how you drive. As I shift out of the metaphor and back to the subject at hand, children are being given the keys of the car at too young of an age, and though there is some debate on what that age should be before handling a smartphone, the research shows that it should not be young children.

We need to give our children a healthy childhood, and screens at an early age are a hindrance not a help. I hope to convince more parents to delay the introduction of screens for as long as possible.

STAGE 2: BEING A MENTOR

My wife and I successfully trained all four of our children to drive and pass the state driver's test to get their licenses. Long before we started the official process by enrolling them in a course once they reached the appropriate age, we took opportunities to talk with them about the importance of safe driving.

Raising awareness about safety became even more pronounced when we knew the time was drawing near for them to start studying for a learner's permit. They had grown up observing Dad and Mom as drivers, but now we needed to become more intentional to explain careful driving habits, such as why it is important not to drive too closely to the person in front of you. Why do we look both ways before making turns? Why do we keep track of the traffic around us by using our mirrors? Why do we pull over when we see the lights of an emergency vehicle behind us? These would all be covered again in the next stage of their pursuit of learning to drive, but parents shouldn't wait until then to begin intentionally teaching their children the rules of the road and how to drive safely when the time came for them to be driving on their own.

Once again, I'm using this as an analogy for the next stage in preparing our children to handle smartphones and the internet. The most crucial point I want to make is that they are not actually using a smartphone or the internet at this stage in their development. But they are being educated about the importance of internet safety and the huge responsibility of handling a smartphone.

Before getting hands-on experience, your children need you to explain why you are not giving them the smartphone to play with and why you are not letting them on the internet to surf the information superhighway. They are certainly going to ask, and this stage of preparation is your opportunity to begin mentoring them.

This approach to equipping your children is the opposite of carelessly handing phones over to them without any prior training. Unfortunately, the heedless approach is the normative behavior in parenting today, but I am advocating for course correction in parenting. Once again, you wouldn't behave this way when it comes to automobiles and driving, so why should parents behave this way with smartphones and the internet?

The late preacher, Matthew Henry, once said the following about child training: "The branch is easily bent when it is tender." The younger the child is, the easier it is to train them for good or for bad. These appetites and habits that are allowed to form at an early age don't decrease as the child gets older; instead, they increase. As they get older, they will become more rigid and sometimes more difficult to work with, but there is a time when they are young that you can more easily influence their environment and activities.

I mentioned Dr. Victoria Dunckley's book earlier, and I highly recommend it. In her practice, she is helping to overcome the problems which often stem from parents heedlessly allowing screen time, especially on smartphones, tablets, and video games. My plea to parents, especially of young children, is to consider the age-old proverb, "An ounce of prevention is worth a pound of cure."

If parents continue to heedlessly give their children smartphones, tablets, game consoles, and access to the internet through computers, they are likely to experience the same results that are presently causing much grief and anxiety in homes today. The Bible teaches that we reap what we sow. What are we sowing into our children's lives?

In the New York Times bestselling book *The Anxious Generation*, the author, Jonathan Haidt, advocates that parents should not give their kids smartphones until high school and should keep them off social media until they are sixteen years old. Whether or not that is the best path forward is one thing, but what should a parent be doing until then, other than just saying no? Training parents to mentor their children in media discernment was not the focus of Haidt's book, but it's the focus of this one.

We need to know why we are saying no, and we need to help our children understand why we are saying no. We can begin to mentor them about their need for a more screen-free childhood and outdoor play as well as preparing them to wisely handle the modern technologies when they are older and wiser.

Another critical component to this phase of training is to give them something better. It's not just about saying no. What are the beneficial things they could be doing instead? Here's the rub, those things are going to cost you more time, money, and energy. The better things for your children are not convenient like turning on the TV or handing them a smartphone, tablet, or gaming device.

I've been teaching this principle for years, in fact, here's my own quote from a book I wrote more than a decade ago, "Unplugging is one step, but filling that new void with something better is the critical follow-up step. The big challenge is that it will take more work. It's convenient to plop on a couch, turn a device on and zone out. It takes more work to plan a craft or an outdoor activity, clear a table to accommodate a puzzle, unearth the board game, put air in the flat tires for a bike ride, plot the journey to the park, assemble the model, fly the kite, read aloud, or endure the process of learning an instrument or listening to someone learn an instrument!"

Here's a personal example from my own family. I said no to video games in our household. That's an honest description, not a prescription for you and your family, though I believe other families could benefit from such a counter-cultural decision without regrets. But what would replace that time for my kids, especially my son who would be more vulnerable to problematic video game use if I had allowed it?

One of the activities I did with my son was build remote-controlled airplanes from scratch and learn how to fly them. This cost me more time, money, and energy than simply giving my son a video game console to consume his childhood and keep him occupied with little involvement from me.

Some screen time was involved because we needed to watch the how-to videos for building and learning to fly these planes. The screen time was minimal, but the process of building these planes from scratch was long and tedious. What excitement we had getting a plane ready for its maiden flight. What grief we shared when we accidentally crashed the plane in our efforts to learn how to control and maneuver the plane effectively in the sky. Unlike video games, there was not a convenient reset button that would allow us to start over without any real-world consequences. We had to take our busted-up plane back into the house and go back to work to repair it and make it flight ready again.

We spent more time building and rebuilding planes than we ever spent flying them, but eventually we got the hang of it and could keep a plane in the air and land it safely.

I didn't share this anecdotal story to compel you to make remote-controlled airplanes with your children; that's not my point. It's just one of many examples of alternatives to screen time. If you would like to try building planes, then I recommend trying it.[3] Some families like to play sports together or go hiking or camping or fishing or hunting. Maybe you like to build with wood or sculpt with clay or make music and learn to play new instruments. There are simple alternatives to screen time, such as board games, cooking together, or riding bikes. My youngest daughter and I became interested in electric scooters, the kind you can rent in urban areas, so I bought a couple of them, and we had many fun excursions together spanning several years.

The challenge is not finding good alternatives to screen time; the challenge is not falling prey to the path of least resistance by defaulting to the convenience of screen time. Sit down as a family and make a list of things you are interested in doing together, set some goals, and then take some action steps.

STAGE 3: THE LEARNER'S PERMIT

I don't know how this stage works in other countries, but in the U.S., the minimum age to get a learner's permit for driving is between fourteen and sixteen years old depending on the state, the average being fifteen across the states. The process varies, but many require students to start a driving course, which begins with learning the rules of the road. They must study for an initial exam to see if they qualify for the learner's permit.

After finishing the course study and taking the exam to receive a learner's permit, the next step is to get a certain number of hours behind the wheel of a car with an instructor. Driving instruction can be part of a school course, or from a private instructor, or oftentimes a parent. For the next six months or up to a year or more, the students will not be driving alone but with responsible adults providing supervision to make sure they are driving safely and following the rules of the road. The goal is to be able to pass a driving examination by the state and receive a license to drive without supervision in the car.

Let's think about how this example could apply to smartphones and internet use by teens. The first thing that may be coming to your mind is, *"You've got to be kidding! The entire process of getting a license to drive is a lot of work and so many steps. How am I supposed to apply this same approach to smartphones and the internet?"* I realize that I'm suggesting a radical paradigm shift in parenting. It's not that it can't be done, but the truth is, many parents don't want the responsibility and the hassle of going through a long and tedious process like driver's ed with smartphones. On top of that, taking your children through a educational course before using smartphones is not required by law, so a parent is not obligated to do it.

I get it, I dreaded the process of helping my teens learn to drive safely, not because I wanted them to be unsafe, but because the whole process required a lot from me, and I'm a busy guy. We opted to do the parent-led driver's course for all our teens, so I've been through the ordeal four times, and each child had a different personality and faced unique challenges to the learning process. The same is the case with handling smartphones and the internet; it's no cakewalk. It's demanding work for the parents, and not always fun for the child. However, the goal is not about having fun or convenience.

It's the arduous work for parents that keeps so many from doing what's best for their children versus what is most convenient for everyone. I'm not trying to guilt anyone or be overly harsh. I'm simply being honest, and I want to challenge you to be brutally honest also. I know you want your child to flourish mentally, socially, physically, and spiritually, yet many parents would prefer that the process could also be convenient and easy. It's not.

What does a learner's permit stage look like for smartphones and teens? I'm going to answer that in the next chapter as I describe four different experiments I conducted in our household as we helped our teens transition from no phones to managing phones with supervision.

STAGE 4: THE DRIVER'S LICENSE

It is truly a milestone in teens' lives when they pass the driver's test and are granted a license with the privilege and responsibility of driving a car on their own. It is no guarantee that they will be collision-free drivers or will never get a ticket for speeding. We hope and pray that they will be defensive drivers, follow the rules, and have extra protection from their guardian angels. As parents, we know unavoidable risks and hazards lie ahead, but we want them to function well in the 21st century, and we celebrate with them as they enter this new stage of life as an emerging adult.

The milestone of demonstrating responsibility should be a similar goal we have in mind for our young adult children with smartphones. We want them to use these new technologies for good and avoid pitfalls, but we want to prepare them to handle adult responsibilities. I don't believe waiting until they are a particular age is enough on its own; our teens need training now.

We need a parental paradigm shift. Our children need brave parents to be trailblazers to set a better trajectory for them because the current trajectory is not working, and the ensuing problems are getting worse. We have enthusiastically welcomed devices into our homes that we thought were cute, but they have now morphed into Gremlins, and they are devouring the family.

ENDNOTES

1. Ari Brown et al., "Media Use by Children Younger Than 2 Years," PEDIATRICS 128, no. 5 (October 17, 2011): 1040–45, https://doi.org/10.1542/peds.2011-1753.

2. David Hill et al., "Media and Young Minds," PEDIATRICS 138, no. 5 (October 21, 2016), https://doi.org/10.1542/peds.2016-2591.

3. https://www.flitetest.com/

CHAPTER 8

MY CHILDREN AS GUINEA PIGS

My kids grew up in a home with a dad who keenly watched the digital migration as it unfolded. I read pertinent books and articles, listened to interviews on radio, watched documentaries, and began writing my own content, and speaking about media and technology from a Christian worldview. No way would my children easily join the migration without cautious parental oversight.

I wanted to try a different approach with my children than ignorantly feeding them to the techno monsters like much of the culture around them. Because there was no clear, alternative path for a counter-cultural parent, I struck out into the techno jungle with its own unknown perils.

In this chapter, I'm going to share my personal journey with my own children. This is a travel log for others embarking on this journey, but it's not intended to be a formula for you. My oldest child became a teen in 2010. According to Jonathan Haidt, 2010 is the beginning of what he refers to as the Great Rewiring of Childhood.

I refer to the period from 2010 to 2015 as the Great Rewiring of Childhood. Social patterns, role models, emotions, physical activity, and even sleep patterns were fundamentally recast, for adolescents, over the course of just five years.[1]

Between 2010 and 2015, the social lives of American teens moved largely onto smartphones with continuous access to social media, online video games, and other internet-based activities. This Great Rewiring of Childhood, I argue, is the single largest reason for the tidal wave of adolescent mental illness that began in the early 2010s.[2]

My last of four children became a teen in 2020. Over the last fourteen years I have conducted four different experiments with my teens on my own parenting journey. You might be thinking, "*Those poor kids!*" But wait until you read the rest of the chapter before you form your opinions and come to any conclusions. When I think about teens and preteens who have been given phones and access to social media indiscriminately by uninformed and undiscerning parents, I am the one thinking, "*Those poor kids!*"

Without ancestral wisdom, I had to navigate the issue of smartphones and parenting on my own, but moving forward, I hope that families can glean wisdom from each other. I want to share the various approaches that I have tried with my kids over the years. These approaches are intended as descriptions that may help, not prescriptions for what you should do. Each experiment had pros and cons. These may be some helpful tools in your toolbox, but there may be other tools you can learn from others that have been equally useful.

EXPERIMENT #1: NO PHONE

My oldest daughter didn't get a smartphone until she was eighteen years old. Was she okay with that? Not really, but by the time she got a phone, she was more mature and appreciative of the responsibility.

She's now a mom with three children, and she doesn't carry regrets about being kept from the smartphone experience during her teen years. My wife and I lent her one of our phones on the occasions that she needed one. In the case of an emergency, she was usually with others who had a phone. We also installed an old school landline so that she could have the wonderful experience of talking with her boyfriend while tethered to a wall in our living room. It didn't hinder their relationship; they've been happily married for eight years now. I should also note that at eighteen, she was responsible for paying for her own mobile service. My daughter was also at liberty to use social media. I thought it was interesting that she opted to stay off of Facebook but did join Instagram and used it carefully. When all was said and done, this experiment worked fine, but I did change my approach for the next ones in line.

EXPERIMENT #2: A SHARED LOANER PHONE

There's nothing wrong with trying something different if you have a thoughtful plan with your child's best interest in mind. I've trained all my children to be young entrepreneurs, and they have had their own small business for over ten years. They had a genuine need to conduct mobile sales transactions and utilize other useful tools on a phone for business. I took one of my retired smartphones and set up a child account through our service provider. They couldn't download any apps without permission from a parent.

One really key point I want to make about my non-adult teens was that I didn't give them this phone, it was mine and I paid for the service. This kept them from thinking I was encroaching upon their space if I checked the contents and activity history on the phone. It was my phone that I was lending to the three of them. They had to share it.

Let me also say that I believe a parent has the right to check the contents of a phone, tablet, or laptop used by their teens. An important piece of advice on this subject is to establish this condition before your teens have access to any technology. You may not imagine any problems at the time, but when they arise and you insist on checking the devices, teens will often cry foul, even though they are mistaken in their cultural ideology about privacy from parents. If you establish this condition for the use of technology up front, it doesn't mean you won't get any pushback, but it will help to remind them that they previously agreed to the terms of service.

This experiment of a shared loaner phone also worked without any major problems in our home.

EXPERIMENT #3: THE SMARTPHONE ALTERNATIVE

A few years ago, I learned about a new phone company called Gabb. Gabb phones[3] look like smartphones but have a tweaked Android operating system that doesn't allow the phone to connect to the internet. They provide GPS location services, calls and texts, and a few useful apps that are preloaded. It has no app store, no social media, no browsing, no video streaming, just the basics. But it still looks cool in the back pocket. My youngest daughter at the age of fourteen began using a Gabb phone for a couple of years and believe it or not, we had zero issues. It sat on the counter most of the time but functioned in the ways we wanted it to function.

Another alternative is the Wisephone by Techless[4]. This company's mission is to help people overcome digital addiction and refocus on relationships. There are no social media apps, and they have tamed the continual distraction of notifications. The phone prioritizes calls, texts, maps, photos, and as an option there are over a thousand vetted apps you can choose from. For parents of kids and teens, there are no workarounds to the safety features. Though I don't have personal experience with this phone, I have several friends who own a Wisephone and they love it. I have affiliate links to both Gabb and Wisephone in the endnotes of this chapter. The small affiliate income from any purchases goes to support my non-profit ministry Media Talk 101.

There's a phone that's even more limited called a Light Phone[5]. It has a colorless screen like a Kindle. It's small but you can call and text, and it has some other utility functions, but no camera, which might be helpful. I know several adults who have switched to a Light Phone to simplify their lives and guard their eyes from tempting content easily found on smartphones. Some people today are opting for older flip phones or other dumb phones to simplify their lives.

EXPERIMENT #4: THE SMARTPHONE

My youngest daughter at the age of sixteen approached me with a two-page document with meticulous bullet points listing a litany of reasons why she wanted me to consider allowing her to have a full-blown smartphone. Most of these reasons had to do with her small business ventures.

She also detailed the guardrails she would agree to follow to have the privilege (not the right) to own a smartphone. It was an impressive document! I scratched off only one thing on her list and added one thing. Are you curious what they were? I said no to Pinterest.

What did I add? She agreed to purchase the phone and pay for the monthly service, but I retained full rights to check the phone at any time or confiscate it if we encountered any major problems. This arrangement worked well without any problems, and now she has graduated from high school and entered adulthood.

I've given you four different ways that we handled smartphones in our home, but those ways don't mean there are no other experiments yet to be tried, I've simply run out of teens in my house, so you'll have to run with the ball now in your home.

I would suggest you consider no phones for young children and tweens. They simply don't need one. Yes, the culture around you will think you're weird and retrograde but just tell your children you love them more than other parents do, and you're not trying to make their life harder, but better. The best is not usually the easiest route forward. Make sure their lives are filled with real life community and activities. The challenge I'm giving is not easy, but it is better.

In the early teens, if there is a need to keep track and stay in contact with your child, then consider Gabb or one of the other alternatives. As they get older, you can consider some of the other ideas I've shared, but the bottom line is that the smartphone can't fill the deepest needs of your child's life. Don't abdicate your critical role in these formative years of your children's lives.

If you open the door to a smartphone in your teens' life, consider establishing it as a loaner phone that doesn't belong to them. Have your children agree to the rules ahead of time and lay out the consequences beforehand if those rules are broken. Getting the arrangement in writing helps, and you can even get your teens to sign it.

MONITORING, FILTERING, AND PARENTAL CONTROLS

With the increasing use of smartphones among teens and now children, more companies are responding to the need for parental controls, monitoring, and content filtering.

I've made my case already the best course is to wait until an appropriate age before allowing your child to use a smartphone. That being said, I also mentioned that when my teen children were sharing a borrowed phone, I used parental controls to stop them from downloading apps without permission and to set times when certain functions would no longer be accessible. It also allowed me to track their location. These were basic tools offered through my phone carrier and IOS.

A plethora of tools is available now for parents that are more robust than what I used. Many apps monitor texts, calls, social media, video games, filter websites, track location, provide geofencing, give activity reports, block apps, pause the internet, schedule screen time, capture screen shots, driving safety reports, and more. I've included a guide at the end of this book in Appendix A: Parent's Guide to Parental Control Apps.

When you research these tools, some of them fall under the category of spyware, but in this case, it is used for keeping watch on what's happening on the phone a child is using. When watching or reading reviews, it's not uncommon to hear reviewers, who are often parents themselves, share their concerns about children's privacy rights.

Okay, let me get something off my chest. If we are talking about children under eighteen years old in the home, the idea of a right to privacy on a device that is purchased by Dad and Mom and the monthly bill paid for by Dad and Mom is ridiculous. I have no idea where this bizarre ideology originated from. It is a parental responsibility to be a shepherd to your children. That watchfulness may not require something akin to spyware, but in my opinion, it is not spying on your children. No, it is monitoring a potentially dangerous access point to harmful content, predators, and scammers. Granted, these types of tools may not be the right fit for other reasons, but I don't buy into the notion that you are somehow being a bad parent for keeping track of what is happening on a phone being used by a child. There you go. I got it off my chest.

In a later chapter, I'll share more about training all my children as woodworkers, but for now, let me add that I was not spying on my children when I hovered over them as they learned how to use dangerous power tools in our woodshop. We can now get back to the subject of tools for monitoring and filtering content.

A few of these parenting tools are free to use, but others cost monthly or annual fees ranging from $3.99/month to $49.99/month. The prices vary depending on the number of devices per plan, and you can get a discounted rate if you pay annually or quarterly versus monthly. I don't want to bog you down with a bunch of details but feel free to refer to the additional content at the end of this book. More of these tools will continue to be developed, so you'll need to do some of your own research to stay on top of emerging options but the guide in the back of this book can help you with the top apps being used at the time of publication. You can also go to YouTube and search "parental control apps for smartphones," and you'll find no shortage of information to slog through.

None of these tools are foolproof, and none of them can replace the need for you as a parent to be present in your child's daily life. These tools cannot do your job of having important conversations or keeping your child's heartstrings tied to you. These helpful apps cannot change your children's hearts or monitor their souls.

They cannot pray for your children or counsel them when they are feeling confused and empty. They will not train your children to be discerning or teach them how and why to make good choices. The bottom line is that these digital tools that provide some helpful guardrails are limited but may be useful in your parenting journey. Don't check out of your other responsibilities as a parent or think that there is a technological solution for every conceivable problem.

In this chapter, I've shared my personal journey of experimenting with different approaches in my own home. Intentionality is key rather than blindly following the cultural current. It may also be helpful for you to know that the experiments in our home with smartphone usage were not carried out in a vacuum that was void of love and grace and the cultivating of family bonds. I'll talk about this more in the chapter Handle with Care. In the next chapter, I will dig into some other tips for taming tech in the home.

ENDNOTES

1. Jonathan Haidt, The Anxious Generation: How the Great Rewiring of Childhood Is Causing an Epidemic of Mental Illness (Penguin, 2024).

2. Haidt, The Anxious Generation.

3. https://gabb.com/ (Affiliate transparency: You can use the code MEDIA for a discount. Proceeds support Media Talk 101).

4. https://wisephone.com?aff=230 (Affiliate transparency: You can use the code mediatalk101 for a discount. Proceeds support Media Talk 101).

5. https://www.thelightphone.com/

CHAPTER 9

TEN TIPS FOR TAMING TECH

I confess, as much as I have embraced technology, some days I wish I could go back to a time before the internet and smartphones when life was simpler. It's wishful thinking and pointlessly vain. The path must be forward not backward, but it shouldn't be a heedless path or a reckless journey.

One of my purposes for writing this book is to help kickstart some deeper thinking about the path forward in our households as we learn how to better handle these technologies without forfeiting our humanity or our need for real community or our spiritual need for communion with God.

This chapter is intended to be inspiring, not comprehensive. I want to encourage you to think deeper about these issues and start taking some steps in a better direction. I hope you will gain wisdom and pass it along to others, and I'm going to demonstrate what that process may look like by passing along some wisdom I've picked up along the way on my own journey of parenting. What

I share will not be enough, and it will come short of answering all the likely problems and scenarios.

Think of the time as a child when you started to learn how to ride a bike, and then the training wheels were removed. An older sibling, a parent, or a friend would hold the bike upright and give it a push as you began to pedal, and off you went. Or down you went. We don't always get it right on the first try. But you must learn to pedal on your own. I'm sure you will scrape your knees in this new chapter of life but don't give up. If you have a crash, get back on the bike and try again. Ready for the first push?

TIP #1: PRIORITIZE PRESENCE

It's not just kids who are distracted by smartphones. Make it a habit to prioritize the people in the room with you and show them that they are more important than your digital connections. It is critical that your children learn from your example. Are you often distracted by your phone? Are your children in competition with your phone for your attention?

I was surprised to come across a novel word for this practice of ignoring your children while distracted by a smartphone. Some have dubbed it "phubbing." It's a mashup of phone and snubbing. Do you snub your children or others in your physical presence by ignoring them while giving preference to someone or something on your phone?

One big step will be to learn how to turn off distracting notifications that are constantly vying for your attention. Mobile operating systems and phone manufacturers will have different ways to change these settings, but you need to educate yourself and learn how to take control of your phone. When you download apps, they often have notifications turned on by default. You may not have paid attention when you were prompted to select your preferences. No problem, you can change that now. Go to your settings and find where to change your notification preferences. Start by turning off all non-essential notifications.

Turn off social media app notifications, YouTube notifications, and Podcast notifications. In fact, you can turn nearly all of them off. I feel like Luke Skywalker when he was about to be crushed in a trash compactor while trying to convince C3PO and R2D2 to shut the trash compactor off. C3PO tells R2D2 to shut them all off.

What should you leave on? Phone calls and texts may be all that you need. It may be more challenging for apps like WhatsApp that serve as a multipurpose tool and can be a mix of essential and non-essential notifications. In some cases, you can limit notifications based on the favorites in your contact list.

Consider removing social media apps from your phone altogether. You can still access them via web browser on your phone if needed or relegate social media to your home computer or laptop. Taking such measures to regain focus is not as extreme as it may sound, and I'm not saying to not use social media, but you don't need it on your phone.

It is important to differentiate between work and play. Many businesses, especially if you are an entrepreneur, require a social media presence and a certain level of social media engagement. The problem with having this on your phone is that it is always with you, even if you are off work. The notifications are likely to suck you into a vortex of distraction from your family.

Companies haven't taken long to create the platforms and apps to train us. We are like highly trained dogs that will respond to the whistle of the trainer. You don't have to let them take control of your life and family any longer. Turn off the notifications to start. It's like robbing the trainer of the whistle that has been used to train you. You might be so well trained that you may question if you have the right to do such a thing. Yes, you can! And you should!

TIP #2: BE A GOOD ROLE MODEL

When it comes to taming tech, one of the biggest hills to climb is to become a good role model for your children. They need help navigating the digital age, and you have the potential to be the best person to provide that guidance. Have you considered how much of their behavior reflects your own?

Young children and teens collect important cues about life through watching Dad and Mom. They may not consciously be thinking about mimicking your actions, but they pick things up for good or bad along the way. You are probably aware of the classic parenting proverb, "More is caught than taught."

It's easy to get frustrated with the way our children interact with smartphones or other devices used for entertainment or media consumption, but are we ready to make needed changes in our own lives before we try to help our teens make needed changes in their lives?

Jesus gave a simple parable about taking the log out of your own eye before trying to take the speck out of a brother's eye. In this case, we have a culture of parents who are blinded by the attraction of smartphones, and we are seemingly not capable of making good judgments for ourselves much less be in a good place to help someone else with their problems.

You may be fully aware of your own bad habits, and you don't want to be a hypocrite to your children, so you don't address those habits in their lives. I'm all for keeping hypocrisy out of parenting as much as possible, but continuing the current course without making any corrections because you don't want to be a hypocrite is not the highest virtue of parenting. The better path is to get things in order in your life so that you can first be a good example to your children.

They really need you to be a mentor, but effective mentoring requires you to model the right behavior first.

TIP #3: PHONE-FREE ZONES

Phone-free zones are good for both places and times. When you are having dinner together, that's both a time and a place not to let phones encroach on this important family time. That small piece of advice brings us to a simple subject that should be part of your overall plan—family dinnertime! So many families are neglecting this important aspect of cultivating a stronger family.

A scene in the Netflix original documentary "*The Social Dilemma*" shows a scripted vignette of a concerned mom making an effort to get her disjointed family together for a family meal, without phones. She repurposed a plastic kitchen safe with a timer meant to lock up cookies to secure everyone's devices for an hour during dinner. The scene shows the awkwardness of a family who does not know what to do with themselves around the table without their phones. Conversation was forced, and the eleven-year-old Isla hears a notification and gets up from the table to check her phone. Her mom tells her the container is locked and to ignore it. As the family attempts to get a conversation going again, it is interrupted by a loud crash as everyone suddenly turns towards the noise and sees that Isla has smashed the container into pieces with a metal tool. They all gape as she grabs her phone and stomps off to be alone in her room. It was a cleverly scripted scene that could easily happen in many homes today, but don't let it scare you from trying.

I wouldn't just spring it on your family without prior communication, but don't hesitate to set boundaries. I'm reminded of a grandmother who shared with me that she keeps a basket at the door to collect her grandchildren's devices when they come over. At the beginning, her grandkids whined and complained but without their phones they were able to have fun playing games and interacting with each other. They made memories that they otherwise would have missed.

As a rule, keeping all screens out of bedrooms is generally a good idea, including smartphones. They are so small and portable that everyone thinks it's okay to take them anywhere and everywhere, but you are the king and queen of your castle, and you can set the rules. As I have already mentioned in a previous chapter, it's easiest to set these rules before a teen has access to a smartphone, rather than try to set up the rule once you start experiencing problems. You have the most leverage as a parent when your teen has not yet been given permission to use a smartphone.

Other phone-free zones might be family vacations, eating out together, during church activities, or visiting family or friends.

TIP #4: WATCH YOUR MEDIA DIET

The biggest challenge for any food diet is self-control. It is also the key to becoming a better athlete. It is also necessary for gaining better control over your media consumption habits. Too often we are being controlled by impulse, cultural pressure, or a lack of goals and direction.

Self-control is the opposite of excess or being out of control. When applied to food, it means that you are not overeating. Moderation takes self-control when applied to media or entertainment, and it means setting limits and sticking to them. It takes discipline to not let it get out of hand in your family. But where do you start and how much is too much? According to the American Academy of Pediatrics, and the American Heart Association, they recommend two hours or less per day for teens.

Granted, there are different ways we interact with screens. Some screen time is essential for work or school. Some is passive entertainment and some for education. Some screen time is for creative purposes like audio or visual content creation. And some screen time is for communication with others. Not all screen time is created equal.

The Bible affirms our need for self-control and gives us an analogy of a disciplined athlete.

> Do you not know that those who run in a race all run, but one receives the prize? Run in such a way that you may obtain it. And everyone who competes for the prize is temperate [exercises self-control] in all things. Now they do it to obtain a perishable crown, but we for an imperishable crown.—1 Corinthians 9:24-25

Most people must be convinced that the effort to exercise self-control is in their best interest. The importance of needed motivation goes back to the subject of your goals and values. You can also find help that goes beyond your own efforts. Let's read what the Bible says about increasing in self-control:

> But the fruit of the Spirit is love, joy, peace, longsuffering, kindness, goodness, faithfulness, gentleness, self-control. Against such there is no law.—Galatians 5:22-23

The fruit of the Spirit is the result of abiding in Christ. Jesus promised that we would receive help through the Spirit of God. Through His Spirit our hearts are changed, and God's laws are written on our hearts. We have a change of heart, and that is better than being governed by external rules. But don't think you're off the hook for developing self-control in your life. Consider the following Bible verse:

> But also for this very reason, giving all diligence, add to your faith virtue, to virtue knowledge, to knowledge self-control, to self-control perseverance, to perseverance godliness.—2 Peter 1:5-6

Do you know what I found to be helpful with developing self-control over my screen time? I make sure my day is filled with better activities. We often default to screen time because it doesn't take as much effort as other things we might be doing and enjoying at the same time. Learn to cultivate self-control in your life and don't give up.

TIP #5: TRADE UP

In 2005, a Canadian blogger, Kyle MacDonald, inspired by a game he played as a kid, dreamed of trading up, starting with a red paper clip, until achieving his goal "for a house. Or an island. Or a house on an island." It seemed like an impossible venture, but after fourteen trades over the course of a year, he successfully traded up for a house.

I love the idea of trading something with less value for something with greater value. Consider trading screen time, which has less value, for things with greater value, such as meaningful family activities: board games, outdoor sports, engaging hobbies, cooking together, crafts, gardening, or any number of non-screen activities. Make a list of things you have been neglecting due to the habit of defaulting to screens. Consider it an investment in the lives of your children.

I encouraged teens for many years to write down five or more activities that they would enjoy doing that doesn't involve a screen. The list may require parents to get involved. Maybe their bike is getting rusty in the garage, or maybe they want to learn to play an instrument, hike a local trail, learn to play tennis, solve a Rubik's Cube, build an RC airplane, learn how to build some wooden shelves, go ice skating, or plant a garden. The possibilities are endless, and each child is a unique person, so what is it that they neglect because of the habit of the diversion of screentime?

TIP #6: DELAY WHEN POSSIBLE

It's easier to keep a door closed for a longer period than it is to shut the door once you've opened it. Once you give a child a smartphone, your parenting becomes much more complicated, and their lives become more troublesome. When problems arise, and they usually do, it is much more difficult to get your parenting going in a better direction than the challenge you may face from delaying the smartphone in your child's life. This principle can apply to many different parenting scenarios, but the smartphone should certainly be delayed as long as reasonable. Granted, the more they are around other kids their age who do not have the same guidance, the more challenging your parenting becomes. Just because it is challenging doesn't mean you shouldn't try. Let's consider some possibilities for meeting that challenge.

I taught my children that other families have different standards when it comes to media and technologies. Each family has the freedom to set those standards whether good, better, or best or poor, careless, or reckless. As a family we are not obligated to conform to another family's standards or lack of standards.

My children also learned that there are families with stricter standards than our own, and I asked them if they wanted me to adjust in that direction? They didn't. I also reminded them that there are families with more lenient standards also. They are not setting the bar for our household.

These conversations became a platform to teach a couple more action steps to take as a family. We were not going to look down on people who had stricter standards, nor judge those who had less. We must function as an autonomous household. Recognizing our autonomy didn't mean I avoided good counsel or refused to learn from others, but at the end of the day, it meant I was accountable to God for directing my family.

I love the story of the Rechabites in the Bible. It's found in Jeremiah 35, and the gist of the story is God tells Jeremiah to invite a family known as the Rechabites to join him at the temple. Then, he was to put wine before them and tell them to drink the wine. Jeremiah did what God told him and guess what happens? The Rechabites refused to drink the wine. Why? Because their father had told them not to drink wine and made abstinence a household rule. That wasn't the only rule. There were other strict rules, and the children and grandchildren kept these rules. God commended them, not for the specific rules, but for their obedience.

> Thus says the LORD of hosts, the God of Israel: Go and tell the men of Judah and the inhabitants of Jerusalem, "Will you not receive instruction to obey My

words?" says the LORD. "The words of Jonadab the son of Rechab, which he commanded his sons, not to drink wine, are performed; for to this day, they drink none, and obey their father's commandment. But although I have spoken to you, rising early and speaking, you did not obey Me."—Jeremiah 35:13-14

A second way to meet the challenge of outside influence is to be choosier about peer group interactions when possible. Limiting peer pressure is not always possible and certainly more challenging for parents with kids in public schools than those in private schools or those who are homeschooled.

Some families take the problem of peer pressure so seriously that they make their educational choices for their children with this and other factors in mind. Bravo for these families. It's not an easy path to put your children through private Christian school or to homeschool them. Microschools, university model schools, or charter schools are also alternatives today. Making important educational decisions is a topic all its own, but it does cross paths with this subject of taming tech in the home.

TIP #7: INTERMITTENT SCREEN FASTS

Earlier in chapter 4, I shared about my first time going on a media fast when I was seventeen years old. I desired to walk closer with God and became uneasy with some of my media choices. At the time, I didn't think my choices had a negative effect in my life, but God was leading me to make some changes.

I planned a two-week media fast and put all my devices and media in a box in my closet. This step I took was early 1990 so my stash consisted of music cassettes, a boombox, and my Nintendo game system. I also avoided television and the movie theater during that time.

Going without electronic media was really hard at first, but in a short amount of time I noticed substantial changes happening in my life because of this break from entertainment. In fact, after two weeks were up, I gladly chose to continue my media fast for a longer period of time. I benefited mentally, spiritually, and emotionally from this break.

A decade later, I was serving as a youth pastor, and it was this positive experience in my own life that influenced me to encourage teens to consider the benefits of a media fast.

The positive experience from my media detox eventually became the catalyst for starting the nonprofit ministry Media Talk 101. My message for teens to take some time to unplug was more than a decade old before it became mainstream to read or hear about the importance of a digital detox.

My own story is not unique for those who have gone on a media fast. I highlighted several stories in my documentary *Captivated: Finding Freedom in a Media Captive Culture*.

TIP #8: ALLOW BOREDOM TO RESULT IN NON-SCREEN ACTIVITY

One of the leading causes of excessive screen time is boredom. When we are bored, we don't know what to do with ourselves, so we have developed a habit of dealing with boredom by gravitating to screens to entertain us. TV, movies, YouTube, social media, and video games have become the default for many people, but it is not a good default. Boredom can be a terrific opportunity for your children to learn to be creative and have fun without screens.

Make sure your children are equipped with non-screen options for play, crafts, reading, and other activities. Don't fall for the incessant whining as if they are going to die if you don't let them default to screentime because it's the path of least resistance. A backyard is also helpful or a park nearby, but you should also plan for indoor discovery time. Your tactics will have to be adapted to your child's age. In time, they may discover that they actually enjoy the screen-free activities when they are given no other options.

TIP #9: CULTIVATE REAL AND HEALTHY SOCIAL NETWORKS

I'll dive a bit deeper into the subject of social media in chapter 11, but for now I want to point out the difficulty of maintaining a large number of digital connections in your life. These superficial acquaintances do not fulfill the need for meaningful relationships. Too often people think they can substitute a few meaningful relationships with a larger group of shallow and superficial online connections. The need for fulfilling friendship can't be pieced together by hundreds of different people. Collecting a pound of pennies will never equal a pound of gold.

Gold is presently around $2,700 per ounce. So, a pound of gold is worth $43,200. The equivalent worth in pennies would require 4,320,000 pennies. One hundred pennies weigh 8.8 ounces. The number of pennies needed to match a pound of gold would weigh 23,760 pounds. Over eleven tons. You couldn't carry it or benefit from it easily. The more social media connections you have, the heavier the burden you bear, with depreciating value when it comes to finding meaning in personal relationships.

Years ago, I became intrigued when learning about something known as Dunbar's Number. The term kept finding its way into news articles and radio interviews in discussions about social media, but what is it?

To quote Wikipedia, "Dunbar's Number is a suggested cognitive limit to the number of people with whom one can maintain stable social relationships, relationships in which an individual knows who each person is and how each person relates to every other person." Dunbar's Number is 150.

Let me give a quick disclaimer, Robin Dunbar is professor of evolutionary anthropology at the university of Oxford, England. He is a naturalist and has an evolutionary worldview. Nevertheless, the data is helpful when considered from a Biblical worldview. His studies have shown that beyond 150 people, humans have a much harder time keeping track of each other.

There's another aspect of our social interactions that some refer to as social layers. One study was done using the phone data from six billion calls by thirty-five million people. In modern slang, there is a maximum of five BFF's or besties in your life in the closest social layer.

The next is your pals, not as close as your besties and that number is ten give or take a few. So now you're up to fifteen.

The next layer outward is your acquaintances, who are around thirty-five people. Now we're up to about fifty altogether. Only five of those are people you are in regular interaction with, another ten less so, then there's the thirty-five who you have less interaction with.

Remember, this is based on phone data not digital social media. You have actually talked with the person. Beyond that fifty, the other hundred in Dunbar's number of 150 are people you rarely talk to but in the course of a year, you may call them, or they might call you at least once.

I realize that this generation has gravitated towards instant messaging and texts for communication. This non-verbal interaction might be your preference, but it is proving to be a substandard way of developing good relationships. Using today's convenient communication shortcuts is a problem if it is the default rather than supplemental to preferred means, like in-person, or a facetime call, or a phone call.

I will share more on this subject in chapter 11, The Suffocation of Social Media. Cultivating a few deep relationships is not only practical and essential for our lives but it was also modeled by Jesus. He taught multitudes of people on occasions, but most of His time was spent with twelve disciples. Out of the twelve, there were three who spent extra time with Him. It looks like Robin Dunbar only lately discovered what Jesus already knew.

TIP #10: TAME YOUR NOTIFICATIONS

In the late 1800's, a Russian scientist named Ivan Pavlov was studying the digestive process in dogs. Sounds like fun, doesn't it? Well, maybe not.

In his research, he observed that dogs started salivating when they could see or smell food. This was a natural biological response, but Pavlov accidentally discovered something he wasn't looking for. He noticed that the dogs started salivating at the sight of his assistant who would usually bring them food, even when he didn't have food to give them.

Don't worry, the dogs didn't want to eat the assistant, but Pavlov discovered that this was a learned behavior, a conditioned response. The dogs associated the presence of the assistant with the arrival of food.

Pavlov diverted his studies and began to experiment with the sound of a metronome. The metronome alone didn't have any effect on the dogs, but then he began feeding them at the same time as the sound. In time, the dogs associated the metronome with food, and just hearing the sound would cause them to salivate even when food was not present.

The habit-forming process is now referred to as classical conditioning in psychology and it also works on humans. So, what does it have to do with smartphones?

We have been conditioned to respond to the vibration or sounds of notifications on our smartphones. You may not start salivating, at least I hope you don't, but there are other physiological responses to this stimulus. You are not anticipating food, so what do you think you'll be getting at the conditioning sound of notifications?

One of the physiological responses happening is a small dopamine hit in your brain. This is a result of an emotional response to the sound of the notification. There is an anticipation of something exciting, or something dreadful, something that makes you happy, or something that makes you sad. It might lead to feeling anxious, or it may result in elation. You may have been waiting to get a response from someone or find out that someone reacted to a social media post, a text, or an email. These anticipated emotions are like the meal that Pavlov's dogs were waiting for. We don't salivate, but our brain triggers the release of dopamine.

When this kind of stimulation continues on a regular basis, you are being conditioned for certain responses. The first is a compulsion to check the notification even if you are doing something else important, such as having a meal with your family or having a conversation with someone in person.

This repeated behavior can lead to habit formation, or habituation. This problem is now referred to as "checking behavior." It is the conditioned response to a conditional stimulus. It can lead to excessive use of your smartphone, habitual distraction, and dependency. It also negatively affects the people around you who are interrupted or ignored because of your conditioned response to phone notifications.

How can you tame your notifications? Simple – turn them off! Go to your settings and take back control over your attention. The same studies also show that you can be "unconditioned" through a process referred to as extinction. Get rid of the metronome altogether or stop feeding the dog every time they hear the metronome. These different approaches are effective at changing the response.

Some notification settings on your phone are set by the app designers automatically to be on rather than off. The app makers know what they are doing. They have studied the psychology of conditioning and are leveraging it for their own purposes. Stop being Pavlov's dogs and don't let others train your behavior.

BONUS TIP: GO GRAYSCALE

Did you know that you can turn the color off on your smartphone and go grayscale? For some people, this simple trick helps them spend less time on their phone. Everything looks bland and less appealing to the eyes, so it becomes a way to retrain your behavior and curtail your phone usage when not essential.

BONUS TIP: ENTERTAINMENT IN COMMUNITY

You can also make better entertainment or recreational choices by watching a movie together as a family instead of everyone being on their own devices and doing their own thing. This has a distinct purpose to cultivate time together. I'm a huge fan of entertainment in community versus entertainment in isolation.

BONUS TIP: SCREEN TIME 101 ONLINE COURSE FOR TEENS

I have adapted much of the content in this book for teens and created a free online course to help you as a parent. There are nineteen short video lessons with follow-along notes, quizzes, and bonus content. You can sign them up at www.ScreenTime101.com today!

BONUS TIP: YOUR DEVICES NEED AN EARLIER BEDTIME

One of the obstacles to sufficient sleep for adults and children is our less than healthy late-night screen habits. I'll explain why in the next chapter, which is all about the importance of a good night's sleep. For now, a simple, but helpful habit is to make sure your electronic devices are put to bed an hour before your children's bedtime.

CHAPTER 10

WHO NEEDS SLEEP?

Many people act as if sleep is overrated—it's not. Sleep is underappreciated. Everyone needs sleep, but children and teens especially are not getting enough. One of the biggest culprits is media, entertainment, and technology. Let me list some of the problems, and then I'll share some solutions and helpful hints for you to consider.

PROBLEM #1

Kids are staying up too late at night fixated upon entertainment or social media. This screen time is cutting into their needed time for better sleep.

PROBLEM #2:

Much of the way children's brains interact with entertainment results in overstimulation late at night when their minds should be winding down instead of throttling up.

PROBLEM #3:

The physical effect of blue light from screens at night triggers a process that keeps children alert when they need to be getting drowsy.

I will unpack these obstacles to good sleep, but first let's look at the effects in their lives when they don't get enough sleep. Everyone needs sleep, especially REM (Rapid Eye Movement) sleep. Dr. Susan Biali Haas writes, "REM sleep is a stage of sleep that is critical for restoration of your mind and body. REM sleep solidifies memories and is tied to your creative and problem-solving skills. If you don't get enough of it, it can leave you feeling groggy and having difficulty concentrating the next day."[1]

Most of you probably have firsthand experience of feeling groggy during the day and struggling to concentrate; I certainly have. Unfortunately, we continue our unhealthy habits that are causing the problems.

The Environmental Health Trust gives some other insight into the subject. "Sleep is a time when the brain cleans out toxins accumulated during the daytime. Ensuring a healthy sleep is one of the most powerful steps we can take to prevent illness and protect our family's health and wellbeing."[2]

The Centers for Disease Control and Prevention has declared that insufficient sleep is a public health epidemic.[3]

Dr. Gary R. Lichtenstein writes, "According to the National Heart, Lung, and Blood Institute, people with sleep deficiency have a greater risk of many health complications, including heart disease, kidney disease, high blood pressure, diabetes, stroke, and obesity."[4]

In an article by Aaron Stevenson published by the American Sleep Association, Stevenson writes, "The first signs you may be aware of when getting less than 6 hours of sleep is you feel tired, forgetful, irritable, and just not on the top of your game."[5]

He also mentions a study done on this subject by the Mental Health Foundation. They found that "people who didn't get enough sleep were four times as likely to suffer from lack of concentration, have relationship problems, are 3 times more likely to be depressed, and 2 ½ times more likely to commit suicide."[6]

He goes on to write about the negative effects on your heart, "The University of Warwick did a study and found that getting less than 6 hours of sleep on a continuous basis makes you 48% more likely to die of heart disease and 15% more likely in developing a stroke. Professor Cappuccio, co-author of the study, said 'The trend for late nights and early mornings is like a ticking time bomb for your health'".[7]

According to the Division of Sleep Medicine at Harvard Medical School, research suggests that sleep plays a vital role in memory, both before and after learning a new task. "It is more difficult to take in new information following a night of inadequate or disturbed sleep. What's more surprising is that it is just as important to get a good night's sleep after learning something new in order to process and retain the information that has been learned"[8]

If your children regularly get a good night's sleep, it positively impacts their mind, their body, and the various systems in their body including their immune system. But how much do they need to sleep each day to get these benefits?

According to the National Sleep Foundation, the recommendation for teens is eight to ten hours every night. Are your teens getting at least eight hours of sleep consistently? If not, let's consider some of the possible disruptors I mentioned at the start of this chapter.

Did you realize that screens emit a lot of blue light? What is blue light anyway? Light has different wavelengths which produce distinct colors, sometimes referred to as color temperature. Blue light is similar to the color temperature of daylight; it is a colder white in contrast with a warm white, and when our eyes are receiving blue light, a process designed by God takes place to tell our brains that it is daytime, and we should be awake and alert.

To get a little more technical, blue light in screens stimulates our eyes and brains which, in turn, suppresses a hormone known as melatonin. Melatonin is part of God's design to help regulate our sleep cycles, technically known as our circadian rhythm—our biological clock. How do you know when to go to sleep and when to wake up? Well, our bodies tell us when we're ready. When melatonin is suppressed by blue light from screens, it suppresses the natural process of winding down and greater readiness for sleep. Blue light is not a bad thing since it is produced by the sun and causes us to be alert, but exposure to artificial blue light also causes us to be alert, when we're not supposed to be.

The problem is that the natural order of things has been upended and now our eyes, and our brains are being affected hours beyond the time that the sun goes down. In ages past, people would light their homes with fire, with oil lamps, or with candles, which all produce a very low and warm light that actually makes you sleepy and signals the brain to start winding down.

Any light source, including warm lighting, can reduce the production of melatonin, but blue light is notorious for stunting melatonin. The technology used to make our screens more energy efficient also produces much more blue light.

A Harvard sleep researcher, Stephen Lockley, points to light at night as one of the reasons many people are getting less sleep than their body needs.

Some experts have recommended setting a bedtime for your devices. Those times range from half an hour to two hours before bedtime so that your melatonin production can be in full effect while you're winding down for bed.

SCREENS AND SLEEP TIPS

Turn on and adjust the night light settings on your phone, computer, or any other device with that functionality. It cuts down on some of the blue light, which can help a little, but not enough to solve all of the problems that come from screens disrupting your sleep.

I wish the following advice was a no-brainer, but don't sleep with your cellphone. In fact, it's best to move all screens out of your bedroom.

It can also help to replace any lights, including night lights, in your bedroom that may emit blue light, such as LED or fluorescent bulbs. Consider using warm incandescent lights instead.

Make sure your alarm clock has a red display instead of white or blue. The red light is less disruptive to your circadian rhythm.

If using a phone as an alarm clock, which I don't recommend because it's better to have your phone away from you at night, put it in airplane mode, sleep mode, or do not disturb mode, to prevent any distractions while sleeping.

Instead of using a backlit screen to read at night, print off articles or read the actual hard copy of books when possible.

Blue light is only one of the problems affecting our sleep when it comes to screens, it is also the lack of self-control to know when to turn your phone off and give your eyes and mind some rest from the constant drip of notifications, videos, posts, and whatever else keeps your eyes engaged late at night.

You've probably experienced being physically tired at night but when you try to go to sleep your mind is racing, and you can't seem to rest. I've heard it referred to as "wired and tired." There are scientific explanations for why your nervous system gets agitated by screen time.

According to Dr. Victoria Dunckley, "Electronic screen devices irritate the brain and overstimulate the nervous system."[9] Dr. Dunckley refers to this growing problem as Electronic Screen Syndrome, or ESS for short. She says, "One way to think about the syndrome is to view electronics as a stimulant (in essence, not unlike caffeine, amphetamines, or cocaine): electronic screen device use puts the body into a state of high arousal and hyperfocus, followed by a 'crash.' This overstimulation of the nervous system is capable of causing a variety of chemical, hormonal, and sleep disturbances in the same way other stimulants can."[10]

This continual connectivity to our devices which cultivates what Dr. Gary Small, author of *iBrain*, refers to as digital fog. It is a form of mental fatigue that is hard to just turn off when you are physically tired and turn off the lights to go to bed. Your mind keeps racing. Dr. Small explains why this happens,

> Our brains were not built to maintain such monitoring for extended time periods. Eventually, the endless hours of unrelenting digital connectivity can create a unique type of brain strain. Many people who have been working on the Internet for several hours without a break report

making frequent errors in their work. Upon signing off, they notice feeling spaced out, fatigued, irritable, and distracted, as if they are in a 'digital fog.' This new form of mental stress, what I term techno-brain burnout, is threatening to become an epidemic. Under this kind of stress, our brains instinctively signal the adrenal gland to secrete cortisol and adrenaline. In the short run, these stress hormones boost energy levels and augment memory, but over time they actually impair cognition, lead to depression, and alter the neural circuitry in the hippocampus, amygdala, and prefrontal cortex – the brain regions that control mood and thought. Chronic and prolonged techno-brain burnout can even reshape the underlying brain structure.[11]

Those are a lot of complicated words describing various regions of the brain that are impacted by techno-brain burnout. But let's talk about something that we can all understand and relate to: your teens are getting less sleep because they stay up too late at night binge watching episodic TV or watching a movie or YouTube videos, playing video games or being glued to social media. Most days, they probably have a set schedule they must follow in the morning, so no matter what time they go to bed, they have to drag themselves out of bed in the morning, under slept and feeling awful.

They might even say to themselves at that moment, "I need to go to bed earlier!" But like most teens, they lack the self-control to make the necessary changes. Self-control is one of the Christian virtues listed in the Bible as a fruit of the Spirit. God wants your children to have this virtue in their life. He knows they need it, but it's an uphill battle in the digital age.

It's not just teens who struggle with self-control; we as parents also have our own challenges. I have a notification set on my phone that goes off every night at 10:30 to remind me to start winding down. I must confess that I often ignore it, especially when I'm watching a movie or episodic show.

The negative effects of the lack of sufficient sleep on your physical, mental, and emotional wellbeing are very real. The scientific studies only confirm what many moms and dads already know intuitively. Your children probably don't know how to set a new trajectory for their life and stick to reasonable boundaries.

The way your children engage with screens, which stimulate parts of the brain, is much different than how their brain handles reading a book, especially in low light. So, try this following tip and see if it makes a difference and helps them get better sleep.

First, help your children set a personal bedtime based on when they have to get up in the morning in order to be ready for school or work and make sure they are getting at least eight hours of sleep. Depending on their ages, they may need more sleep than that. The next step is to walk the time back at least an hour before their bedtime to be free from screens.

To put it simply, be sure all devices have a bedtime that is at least an hour before theirs.

Then, encourage them to keep their lights on low, pick up a good book, and read in bed. Now, they may be wired differently, but if I'm tired, reading a book will put me to sleep in minutes. Try this routine for a week and see if they sleep better and wake up more rested.

ENDNOTES

1   Susan Biali Haas MD, "Using Your Phone at Night Will Make You Sleep-deprived and Exhausted. Really.," Psychology Today, April 17, 2018, https://www.psychologytoday.com/intl/blog/prescriptions-for-life/201804/6-ways-that-night-time-phone-use-destroys-your-sleep.

2   "Screens and Sleep - Environmental Health Trust," Environmental Health Trust, September 2, 2022, https://web.archive.org/web/20231208043159/https://ehtrust.org/key-issues/cell-phoneswireless/screens-and-sleep/.

3   Julia Rodriguez, "CDC Declares Sleep Disorders a Public Health Epidemic," Advanced Sleep Medicine Services, Inc., December 9, 2016, https://www.sleepdr.com/the-sleep-blog/cdc-declares-sleep-disorders-a-public-health-epidemic/.

4   Gastroenterology & Hepatology, "Letter From the Editor: The Importance of Sleep - Gastroenterology &Amp; Hepatology," December 22, 2015, https://www.gastroenterologyandhepatology.net/archives/december-2015/letter-from-the-editor-the-importance-of-sleep/.

5   American Sleep Association, "How Important Is Sleep for the Body & Mind? | American Sleep Association," June 14, 2021, https://web.archive.org/web/20220705062142/https://www.sleepassociation.org/about-sleep/how-important-is-sleep/.

6   Ibid.

7   Ibid.

8   "Sleep and Memory," Sleep Medicine, n.d., https://sleep.hms.harvard.edu/education-training/public-education/sleep-and-health-education-program/sleep-health-education-88.

9   Victoria L. Dunckley MD, Reset Your Child's Brain: A Four-Week Plan to End Meltdowns, Raise Grades, and Boost Social Skills by Reversing the Effects of Electronic Screen-Time (New World Library, 2015).

10 Ibid.

11 Gary Small and Gigi Vorgan, iBrain: Surviving the Technological Alteration of the Modern Mind (Harper Collins, 2009).

CHAPTER 11

THE SUFFOCATION OF SOCIAL MEDIA

I wonder if an ancient proverb can shed light on the challenges we face today with social media platforms? The proverb says, "Seldom set foot in your neighbor's house, lest he become weary of you and hate you" (Proverbs 25:17).

Social media allows us to be in other peoples' business at any given moment. It's not like you are showing up at their house unannounced or uninvited. It is more like their door is wide open for you to walk right in, except if you were to enter their home in real life and not online, you might not recognize the person or the environment. Social media is not necessarily presenting real life, with all the flaws, the insecurities, the fears, the doubts, the hidden compartments of the soul, and longing to be affirmed and validated, sometimes to the point of desperation.

In this chapter, I aim to speak not only to parents concerned about their children's interactions with social media but to all of us. I hope you will be encouraged to think deeply not only about your children and social media but also how many of these issues apply to adults as well. Children and teens are in a more vulnerable stage of life when interacting with social media. Their mental, emotional, and spiritual formation is tender and still taking root like new plants emerging in a spring garden. Social media can be like a dog fight in the middle of a newly planted garden. The young plants get ripped up by their shallow roots and they wither.

As adults, we have mental, emotional, and spiritual roots that have grown deep like a tree and help us weather the storms. Even so, adults also struggle sometimes with handling social media with maturity and wisdom.

It's easy for adults to forget how things that we would deem trivial today were once monstrous issues when we were teens. Social media amplifies these issues for teens and preteens.

God has made us social beings. Yet, because of our sinful nature and our tendency towards extremes, we may find ourselves intentionally isolating ourselves or always being around others without personal time for quiet and reflection. Social media caters to both those extremes at the same time. Even if we think we are connecting socially online, this type of connection is disembodied social engagement, meaning we are not in each other's presence. It is an experience we have in isolation. Disembodied means that a physical person is not present.

The meaning of being social has been hijacked. The authentic definition has been abducted and replaced with an imposter. The use of the word "social" should probably be removed from "social media" if we are merely interacting with a screen. It is not social if we are viewing curated content and not interacting in person. The original meaning of being social, before electronic media, was never imagined as something disembodied.

I realize the term "social media" is here to stay, I'm advocating that those longing for authentic and meaningful social interaction understand that online social media is an illusion or, at best, a shadow of what we were created to experience in society with others.

Technology can be used for simultaneous, real-time interaction with another person through phone calls, video calls, and instant messaging. These methods are still disembodied, but they have greater value than passively viewing posted content. Not all screen time is created equal.

The ability for people to communicate simultaneously while not in person is a relatively new phenomenon in human history. It began with the invention of the telegraph, the grandfather of telephones, radio, television, and the internet.

I mentioned Marshall McLuhan in chapter 6 and his philosophy about the extensions and amputations of mankind through modern technologies. The telegraph and subsequent technologies were certainly extensions of mankind and revolutionary in history. We often neglect analyzing and scrutinizing what has been amputated or left behind in these technological leaps forward. Let's consider the benefits of regaining focus on in-person social interactions.

It helps to consider Jesus, the Son of God. Jesus didn't project Himself into our world, He became flesh and dwelt among us. His Father could have chosen to send Him in this technological age of screens and broadcasting, but He didn't. He was sent in an era before the invention of the printing press. He came in person and interacted with a finite number of people in His short lifetime on Earth. He had twelve men who were closer to Him than any others, and three who were closer still among the twelve. After His death and resurrection, the one-hundred and twenty faithful followers gathered in Jerusalem to pray and wait for the next chapter to be opened.

As we consider the illusion of today's social media, we can learn something from the Son of God, who could have planned an appearance seemingly less limited than being born to an insignificant family in a small town and living among unknown and uncelebrated people. He remained in obscurity until His baptism at about the age of thirty and spent the next three or so years in the spotlight and in person. He sometimes attracted thousands of people to hear Him teach, but most of His limited time on Earth was spent with a small group of people. We should aspire to follow in His footsteps.

Interacting with others in person can be unpredictable. We may do our best to look good, speak well, impress others, but it is in real time, and we can't control what others may say or do or other variables out of our control. A short story from my own archives illustrates this point.

When in grade school, I liked a girl named Heidi, and during lunch one day while sitting across from her, I attempted a new method of getting ketchup out of the small packet through using a tine of a fork to pierce a hole toward the top. I learned this from another boy, and squeezing out a fine stream onto your school lunch tray seemed cool. In my attempt to impress Heidi, I never imagined in a moment that the trajectory of the ketchup stream would not hit the tray as planned. Instead, it had a mind of its own and shot straight across the table and hit Heidi's beautiful sweater. She could not be convinced that the ketchup blast was an accident, but it was. Talk about a Charlie Brown moment. Social interactions are risky, even in grade school. No wonder we would rather curate our image if possible.

How social is social media anyways these days? I've already made the case that the word social is mislabeled, but the supposed "social" elements are eroding on the platforms, thin as they were already. Paid posts from strangers, influencers, and companies with something to sell now seem to dominate the space. Feeds are inundated with memes, click bait, sales funnels, schemes, and low content videos with a tendency to amuse the user. Content is increasingly more controlled by the platforms through algorithms and paid content. Many of these posts are intentionally appealing to the base voyeuristic inclinations of humanity. They intend to amuse, shock, or tug on the sinful nature in an effort to grab attention for their own agenda. Much of the paid content or trending posts appeal to our tendencies to be drawn to novelty. Marketers know how to tap into our deep longings and present a temporary vicarious experience. We are given an illusion and the emotion of thinking we have come near to someone. Maybe someone we know in person, but often someone we don't know. Someone famous, someone notable, someone idolized.

Even if you would like to see content from an actual friend or acquaintance on social media, seeing it is becoming more difficult. It's like driving across town to go meet a friend, but the streets have been barricaded, and you are forced into a detour. Along the route, you are forced to stop at checkpoints, and in the end, you never get to your friend. There are also distractions along the way that are not forced stops, but moments when you easily become diverted by eye-candy, voyeur-bait, curiosity traps, lust magnets, tease reels, crass landings, and fool's fodder. None of it is "social" media. It's just diverting amusement. Amuse means "to not think."

Social media can be a wonderful tool when used carefully and intentionally with wisdom. Unfortunately, the more teens spend time on social media, the more anxious, depressed, and sometimes suicidal they become according to research. Why is that so? One of the many contributors affecting the mental health crisis among young people today is what is referred to as *upward comparison*.

Let me explain *downward comparison* first. Downward comparison is comparing yourself with someone who is below you according to the app's methods of keeping track of popularity through likes, follows, shares, and comments. You look at someone else's profile and posts and see that they don't get as many likes, they don't have as many followers, and the comments they receive are fewer or more negative. Your own ego and sense of worth is boosted by the knowledge that you are more popular than someone else.

Upward comparisons are in the other direction. You see yourself as less popular than others based on their quantified popularity. Quantified popularity means you can add it up: they have more followers than you, they get more likes than you, they receive more positive affirmation in comments than you, and so on. Their popularity is quantifiable like points in a game. The person with the most points is better than you. It makes you feel unpopular, unloved, and unimportant, no matter how hard you try to get more attention. Upward comparison often leads to anxiety and depression.

It's hard to get attention because the market of social media is saturated. There will always be profiles that gain popularity and give the false hope that maybe someday it will be you who becomes popular, and maybe you'll finally feel liked, appreciated, and important once you achieve some level of prominence in your social network.

Let me tell you something that can be life changing for you and your children if you take it to heart. Your worth, your value as a person, is not defined by popularity on social media no matter how much pressure from culture tries to convince you otherwise. Not enough people in your life are telling you or your children this important truth. If you merely march along with the crowd, you will find yourself empty if you haven't found your identity in something eternal instead of fleeting popularity.

Cultivating a few close friends rather than a hundred or a thousand superficial social media connections is intrinsically more valuable in your life. And it is eternally more valuable to cultivate your relationship with God who gave you life and gives you worth.

Social media can be a useful platform for broadcasting helpful information to others if your understanding of worth is not defined by responses from others on the platform.

Another concern with online social media is how the entire system has been gamified through follows, likes, comments, and shares. Gamification in social media is what allows for quantified popularity, like keeping score in a video game. This system is designed to gauge popularity but not to help your personal well-being. If you are not secure in your identity outside of your social media presence, quantifiable metrics are going to be greater obstacles for you.

Big Tech doesn't care about your personal well-being; they care about getting more of your attention on their apps, just as a game designer works hard to keep players engaged in the game. Why? They are making you and your time a product to be sold to advertisers.

The reality of your screen time attention being a commodity for social media companies was demonstrated clearly in the Netflix original documentary *The Social Dilemma*. If you already have a subscription, I recommend you sit down with your family and watch it. It is eye-opening when you hear from former employees and designers of these apps. They don't hesitate to reveal that the systems they built are designed to make your attention a product to be sold.

I began speaking about social media, starting with MySpace in 2003 and afterwards, Facebook in 2005 during the early days of their introduction into mainstream culture. I sometimes felt like a lone voice of caution. Parents and sometimes a teen would ask, "What do you think about Facebook?" I set up my own profile early on to try and understand it. Even then, I was asked when posting, "What's on your mind?"

That's quite a question to ask when you are about to broadcast to the world what is on your mind. A more important question to ask would be, "Is your heart in the right place? Is it in alignment with God?" The potential problem of amplifying your thoughts on social media platforms is brought to light in the following words of Jesus,

> For a good tree does not bear bad fruit, nor does a bad tree bear good fruit. For every tree is known by its own fruit. For men do not gather figs from thorns, nor do they gather grapes from a bramble bush. A good man out of the good treasure of his heart brings forth good; and an evil man out of the evil treasure of his heart brings forth evil. For out of the abundance of the heart his mouth speaks.—Luke 6: 43-45

What you post is the fruit from your tree, the manifestation of what is really in your heart. If your heart is not governed by God's Spirit, if it has not been transformed by the gospel, if it has been poisoned by deception and sin, then what you post is going to be bad fruit.

On the positive side, if your heart is submitted to God, if it is being transformed by His Spirit, and you are full of life through the gospel of Jesus Christ, then your social media posts will reflect a good heart which produces good fruit. Your social media posts can be used to inspect your heart: is it in the right place or the wrong place? What is inside is going to make it outside by what you communicate, and these are merely platforms for broadcasting what comes out of your heart. Or as an old saying goes, "What's in the well comes up in the bucket."

I'm going to share more about the heart in a future chapter, but for now, if your heart is confused, sinful, angry, cynical, or vindictive, it's going to manifest in your life with or without online social media. When you add social media platforms to the mix, it is like taking an electric guitar and plugging it into a huge amp and then turning the volume up all the way. It's not merely a reflection of your heart—it's an amped broadcast.

If your pastor (and I hope you have at least one in your life) was to visit your Facebook, Instagram, or X profile, what would he find? An advertisement for the world? Or a reflection of Christ shining through you? If your social media posts reflect the world and not Christ, I recommend you get your face into God's book until you begin to reflect Him and not the world. Once you are reflecting Christ and are a good example to the face-to-face relationships in your life, then by all means amplify Christ through whatever means are available to you.

CHAPTER 12

THE SUFFOCATION OF SOCIAL MEDIA: PART 2

Another growing challenge with social media is being chained to your device and constantly distracted from the tangible world around you. There is often a suffocating effect from the pressures of keeping up with social media. The anticipated benefits from maintaining your online image can be outweighed by the costs paid through stress and anxiety.

If you thought of your soul as a fuel tank, what is filling it and what is draining it? If social media truly filled your tank, then why do you need to come back to it so often? I fill the fuel tank in my car about once a week, and then I drive around until the low fuel light comes on. What does your constant attachment to social media tell you? It tells you that it is draining your soul more than filling it. The larger your online social circle grows the amount of anxiety also grows because it's draining you but not filling you up.

I remember the emergence of the virtual pet craze in the mid-nineties beginning with the Tamagotchi virtual pet, followed by Digimon, Giga Pets, Nano Pets, and others. If you are not familiar with any of these, they were a keychain sized toy that fit in your pocket with a tiny LCD screen portraying a low bit animation of your pet and a few buttons for interactions. These required regular intervals of care and attention. If you neglected your virtual pet or monster, it became weaker and would eventually die, but if you spent more time with it, then it would thrive.

It was stressful, and compelled kids to stay connected to the device in their pocket. The virtual pet eventually moved online with a much more robust user experience with better graphics and a huge increase into the scope of the pet's world. It had tremendous success at keeping kids glued to a computer to keep up with their Neopets.

Now, imagine how this relates to your social media connections today. It is one thing if you have only a single friend online to invest time with for the purpose of cultivating your relationship. What would the effect be for a child who didn't have just one Nano Pet in his or her pocket but a hundred or more? It would be a full-time job trying to maintain the connection to each virtual pet. Along with the time needed, anxiety and stress would also increase. Many teens today are encountering a compound problem—the paradox of being driven to boost their self-image by having more social media connections but becoming more anxious and depressed as those connections grow and have to be managed.

Teens have struggled for decades with bullies, cliques, being unpopular, and longing for popularity. Long before the digital age, cultivating one or more meaningful friendships was challenging work. Finding and keeping friends was stressful back in my day, but it does not compare to the out-of-proportion expectations that are put on teens today in their online lives. There are expectations of themselves and expectations from others. It has become a suffocating oppression that weighs upon this generation.

These expectations, which resulted in a growing amount of stress and anxiety, became apparent in the rise of the texting culture. Before social media took deep root, and social media platforms like Twitter emerged, there was already a growing problem known as hyper texting. Along with the overwhelming number of texts being sent and received by teens came unrealistic expectations of responding to received texts immediately; otherwise, your friendship or devotion would be in question. Friends might doubt your loyalty or friendship with them if you didn't respond right away. These unrealistic expectations, which I have coined as *text-pectations,* changed youth culture and built a new foundation that has kept teens more devoted to a relationship with their devices than they are devoted to cultivating healthy in-person relationships.

This behavior, conditioned by the expectations of the culture, can also impact a person's relationship with God. For example, if you expect instantaneous responses from your friends as proof of their love and devotion, what do you think is going to happen when you decide to spend a few minutes praying to God, and He doesn't answer you immediately? Are you going to doubt His love and concern for you? Many do because they are conditioned by these shallow and unrealistic expectations that others must respond immediately because you took the time to message them. God has made it clear in the Bible that He loves you and cares about you, but He does not always answer your prayers immediately. He allows this time of waiting and silence for your own good.

Jesus gave a parable about a widow and a judge and explained that His purpose was to encourage people to pray persistently and not lose heart when they didn't get an immediate answer from God.

If you or your teens are struggling with our culture's expectations to always respond quickly to every post, message, or text, would you like to find freedom? You can! Your kids can! Many teens today are making a choice to unplug from online social media altogether or are finding ways to use it with wisdom. We've already discussed several possible action steps to have a more balanced media diet in your family, so are you really wanting to take better care of them? You can with God's help. If non-Christian teens are learning how to do it without looking to God for help, how much more will your teens be able to thrive with God's help and the support of Dad and Mom?

I've already covered a sufficient list of concerns that should be food for thought in the days and years ahead, but there's more. In an earlier chapter, I talked about the problem of sleep deprivation and bad habits negatively affecting good sleep. Social media is one of the big culprits for keeping teens up past a reasonable bedtime in order to manage their digital connections. It is a more powerful draw than a virtual pet in your pocket because the social world changes every day, every hour, every minute.

When it comes to upward comparison, this often cultivates envy, jealousy, and strangely enough, loneliness. How can having 24/7 connections to online friends result in more loneliness? Remember my fuel tank analogy? The shallow connections online don't meet the deepest needs that your children have for face-to-face community.

Another symptom and problem with the new methods of communication is the inferiority of online communication and the faceless path to being mean when interacting online. Face-to-face communication comes with facial expression, tone of voice and other non-verbal cues that cannot be sufficiently replaced with emojis. Being pithy and writing short coherent content is not a skill that most people have developed. In the meantime, we have a generation not fully developing face-to-face social skills. It is easier to be cruel to someone online when they are not directly across from you in person. Your attempts at being funny or sarcastic may not translate online the way you intended.

I realize that this generation's habits of communication have gravitated towards instant messaging and texts, which are non-verbal. Though it might be your preference, it is proving to be a substandard way of developing good relationships if it is the default rather than supplemental to more preferred means, like in-person, a facetime call, or a simple phone call.

Believe it or not, there's still more to think about, including the growing trend of risky, dangerous, and often regrettable online challenges. Social media trends have ushered in peer pressure 2.0, and it is driven, once again, for the desire to be affirmed, to be validated by peers, and living on likes, while falling prey to toxic comparisons. Pointing out yet once again, the need for your children to find their identity in Christ and not in their online presence.

Let me bring this chapter to a conclusion by showing you how the ancient wisdom of Biblical proverbs can be applied to the unique issues we are considering. Take these to heart and pass them along to your children.

Proverbs 10:19 says, "In the multitude of words sin is not lacking, but he who restrains his lips is wise." If you applied this proverb to social media, it would mean that you would be wise to be more restrained on what you post and how often. Less is more. More wisdom.

Proverbs 17:27 is similar. "He who has knowledge spares his words, and a man of understanding is of a calm spirit." It takes knowledge and understanding to spare your words and not get riled over something someone else says or posts. You can stay calm—it is more mature. The less mature person just blurt things out.

Proverbs 16:24 says, "Pleasant words are like a honeycomb, Sweetness to the soul and health to the bones." When you do post on occasion it should be something that builds others up not tears them down. There's enough of that already in the world. Bring health to others through social media, not hurt.

Here's one of my favorites, Proverbs 12:18 (NASB): "There is one who speaks rashly like the thrusts of a sword, but the tongue of the wise brings healing." A vivid picture has been painted in this proverb. It gives us the image of a careless person with a sharp sword foolishly swinging it around. Someone's going to get hurt needlessly. When you are careless, when you are rash with your words, online or in person, you are likely to harm another person. On the other hand, the proverb also tells us that when you use wisdom, then your words can bring healing to hurting people.

Proverbs 18:7-8 tells us, "A fool's mouth is his destruction, and his lips are the snare of his soul. The words of a talebearer are like tasty trifles, and they go down into the inmost body." Gossip is eaten up like candy or salty chips, but it is poisonous. It may get attention on social media, but it's not right; it hurts everyone. Not only is there a problem with being bombarded with foolish, meaningless, or mean and caustic words from others in their posts, comments, and messages, there is the tendency to follow suit and do the same to others.

There is a great need for words that bring life and healing. Words are powerful. They can do harm, but they can also heal. Proverbs 15:4 says, "A wholesome tongue is a tree of life, but perverseness in it breaks the spirit." There are people that try to break the spirit of others through their meanness. It's better to bring life to others by what you post online.

Proverbs 17:4 says, "An evildoer gives heed to false lips; A liar listens eagerly to a spiteful tongue." Here's another problem. When you post things that are spiteful, or things that are lies, you only attract evildoers.

The next Proverb is about guarding your mouth. In this case we are talking about guarding what you post online. Proverbs 21:23 says, "Whoever guards his mouth and tongue keeps his soul from troubles." You will keep yourself from unnecessary trouble if you guard what you post online.

The next example is from Psalms 141:3. This Scripture is a prayer, asking God for help. Memorize this! It says, "Set a guard, O LORD, over my mouth; keep watch over the door of my lips."

Let me close this chapter with one more passage from the Bible that digs deep into the subject of what comes out of your mouth. It applies to what you post online, and it was written by James, the half-brother of Jesus.

> All of us often make mistakes. But if a person never makes a mistake in what he says, he is perfect and is also able to control his whole being. We put a bit into the mouth of a horse to make it obey us, and we are able to make it go where we want. Or think of a ship: big as it is and driven by such strong winds, it can be steered by a very small rudder, and it goes wherever the pilot wants it to go. So it is with the tongue: small as it is, it can boast about great things. Just think how large a forest can be set on fire by a tiny flame! And the tongue is like a fire. It is a world of wrong, occupying its place in our bodies and spreading evil through our whole being. It sets on fire the entire course of our existence with the fire that comes to it from hell itself. We humans are able to tame and have tamed

all other creatures—wild animals and birds, reptiles, and fish. But no one has ever been able to tame the tongue. It is evil and uncontrollable, full of deadly poison. We use it to give thanks to our Lord and Father and also to curse other people, who are created in the likeness of God. Words of thanksgiving and cursing pour out from the same mouth. My friends, this should not happen! No spring of water pours out sweet water and bitter water from the same opening. A fig tree, my friends, cannot bear olives; a grapevine cannot bear figs, nor can a salty spring produce sweet water.—James 3:2-12 (GNB)

Your words are powerful and can harm others or help others. If you are going to use social media platforms for communication, make sure you are a blessing and not a burden to others who will see what you post. I'm an enthusiastic fan of people using social media to promote the truth of God's word and encourage others to keep their eyes on Christ. May your communication be a spring of life-giving water to others.

CHAPTER 13

THE DARK SIDE OF SCREEN TIME

To be honest, I didn't want to write these upcoming chapters. In over twenty years of teaching about screen time habits and pitfalls, I have intentionally focused on common problems found in most households. I've avoided using sensational stories to motivate parents to set boundaries in homes. There are enough good reasons to set these boundaries without using fear tactics. Unfortunately, the occasional shocking news stories twenty years ago are now being eclipsed by dark and disturbing trends disrupting more and more homes today.

Revenge porn, sextortion, online predators, AI sexting chatbots, screen addictions, teen depression, suicidal thoughts, and self-harm fueled by online activity are just some of the growing issues families face today.

The darker side of screen time is invading more homes, and its ominous shadow is reaching more children through smartphones, tablets, and laptops. Children's bedrooms were once safe spaces, guarded by parents and filled with stuffed animals, LEGO sets, *Highlights* children's magazines, crayons, and coloring books. But now the bedrooms are hosts to portals leading to a dark underworld hiding behind each glowing screen. Children find open doors and dimly lit paths into the darkest recesses of our culture. Children are lured by deceitful tactics that exploit their natural curiosity, ignorance, and innocence.

Many of the subjects in this chapter are now commonly highlighted in today's news. In the last month, I've heard about Facebook's AI chatbots sexting with supposed children,[1] the FBI targeting a global sextortion ring following a series of teen suicides[2], and an interview with a former recruiter of OnlyFans porn accounts for young women[3].

I really don't like delving into these subjects and it's probably safe to say that most parents don't either. The purpose in writing this chapter is to remind us to have reasonable safeguards, age-appropriate conversations, and open lines of communication so that our kids know they can come to us and find refuge in a time of desperation. We can hope that there will be no reason to have these conversations, but the dark side of screen time and the schemes of the devil do not ask permission first before setting such heart-wrenching traps for kids.

I could wait to give you helpful action steps after I shed some light on the dark realities, but instead, I believe it would be helpful to share some action steps now and repeat them at the close of this section. My call to action is to encourage you to implement a comprehensive family plan to keep your kids safe. Let me suggest what this might look like using the acronym **GRACE**: GUARDRAILS, RULES, AWARENESS, CONVERSATIONS, and ESCAPE ROUTES.

GUARDRAILS are the technology options available to you for monitoring and blocking content. It also includes limited and age-appropriate access to technology. Don't skip over Appendix A at the end of this book.

Rules are just that—household rules. They are decided by you, the parents. They are for your children's safety and wellbeing, not because you want to make life more difficult for them or for you. Good rules exist for good reasons.

Awareness is teaching your children about *why* you have guardrails and rules. Help them to understand your reasoning based on your love for them and having their best interests at heart.

Conversations are ongoing discussions. Make screen time a regular subject of discussion in your family and have age-appropriate talks about the common traps of the dark side. Hopefully, you are already convinced of the benefits of delaying access to the internet and smartphones for your younger children. When they get older and begin using phones and the internet, they are also old enough for you to broach these conversations. When you hear a media related story in the news that affects children, be sure to talk about it. When a Public Service Announcement (PSA) is issued for the safety of children, use the opportunity to keep the conversation going.

Escape routes are predetermined safety nets. If the above safety measures fail, or if they are neglected, and your child finds themselves in online trouble, they need to know without question that it is safe to come to you without fear. The worst thing that could happen is they get trapped in a scheme and hide it from you for fear of getting in more trouble. The time to teach your children to come to you if they find themselves in trouble is not after the trouble has cornered them.

Let's quickly review the acronym **GRACE**: **G**uardrails, **R**ules, **A**wareness, **C**onversations, and **E**scape routes. The acronym is a helpful reminder that this family action plan is about love, not law. It's loving and gracious to protect your children from prevalent dangers while they mature and learn how to protect themselves.

The following subjects are not covered in a comprehensive manner. They are a general overview of known dangers troubling households today. Far from fearmongering, addressing these difficult subjects is a needed wake-up call to parents. I'm going to start with pornography because it fuels our hyper-sexualized culture, which drives much of the dark side of screen time.

ENDNOTES

1. Jeff Horwitz, "Meta's 'Digital Companions' Will Talk Sex With Users—Even Children," The Wall Street Journal, April 26, 2025, https://www.wsj.com/tech/ai/meta-ai-chatbots-sex-a25311bf.

2. Josh Campbell, "'Sextortion' Ring Targeting Thousands of Minors Worldwide Was Just Disrupted by the FBI, Officials Say," CNN, May 15, 2025, https://www.cnn.com/2025/05/15/politics/sextortion-ring-distrupted-ryan-last.

3. "Morning Wire." Interview by Megan Basham. Daily Wire, May 10, 2025, https://www.dailywire.com/episode/it-s-all-a-lie-former-only-fans-insider-reveals-dirty-secrets-member-exclusive.

CHAPTER 14

THE DARK SIDE OF SCREEN TIME: PORNOGRAPHY

According to research conducted by Common Sense Media, their 2022 report, *Teens and Pornography*,[1] gives the following statistics:

- 15% said they first saw online pornography at age 10 or younger. The average age reported is 12.

- 54% of children 13 or younger have seen pornography online.

- 73% of children 17 or younger have seen pornography online.

- 44% have seen it intentionally. Additionally, 58% have seen it accidentally.

- 71% who said they have intentionally watched pornography reported viewing it in the last week.

- Unintentional exposure to pornography could be a common experience for teens, as 63% of those who said they have only seen pornography accidentally reported that they had been exposed to pornography in the past week.

- 45% felt that online pornography gives helpful information about sex.

- Roughly one in three (31%) who said they had viewed pornography while attending school in person. Furthermore, among teens who reported that they have viewed pornography during the school day, nearly half (44%) reported having viewed pornography on school-owned devices.

- A majority of teens who indicated they have viewed pornography have been exposed to aggressive and/or violent forms of pornography. This includes 52% who reported having seen pornography depicting what appears to be rape, choking, or someone in pain.

- 57% of teens have not discussed pornography with a trusted adult.

- 50% of teens said they "feel guilty or ashamed after watching online porn."

- Among all teens responding to the survey, slightly fewer than one in three (32%) said there are currently content filters or parental controls in place at their home to try to prevent them from accessing pornography.

Your children don't need to be looking for pornography online to be exposed to it. They may misspell a word in a browser search bar and naively fall for clickbait or get hooked through a sophisticated phishing scheme. Porn peddlers are looking for them and using all the effective marketing tactics of online funnels at their disposal.

Understanding why perpetrators target children when they have plenty of adult consumers already is perplexing. It's a multi-billion-dollar industry with global annual revenues reaching nearly sixty billion. The Bible tells us in 1 Timothy 6:10, "For the love of money is a root of all kinds of evil." A spiritual battle is also raging between good and evil in addition to the corruption of unregenerate hearts. Long before photos, videos, the internet, and smartphones, we are given an indictment from heaven about the state of mankind, "Then the LORD saw that the wickedness of man was great in the earth, and that every intent of the thoughts of his heart was only evil continually" (Genesis 6:5).

Perverted minds and warped hearts plot and scheme to satisfy twisted lusts. It is like a plague that spreads through society. People are usually not content to keep sin to themselves. They have a distorted sense of justification if others are also participating and a disdain for those who don't go along. The problem of calloused sinners enticing others to join them in sin was already happening in the first century and evident in the words of the apostle Peter who wrote, "They are surprised when you do not join them in the same flood of debauchery, and they malign you" (1 Peter 4:4 ESV).

The magazine pictures from thirty years ago were bad enough but not usually accessible to most children unless irresponsible adults were involved. X-rated movies were often confined to seedy roadside stores with age restrictions for access. All this changed with the internet. We now live in a world with ubiquitous access to porn through smartphones anytime and anywhere. The convenient accessibility also accounts for the massive financial boon to the growing porn industry.

Pornography is destructive and addictive. It continues to descend into deeper, darker recesses of human depravity through child trafficking, sexual violence, and other perversions which supply the growing demands from desensitized consumers. These consumers are getting younger and younger due to early exposure.

This dark underworld has unfortunately existed long before smartphones, but the majority of children were shielded from exposure to it or from becoming victims of it. That's no longer true. The majority of children with unsupervised access to the internet are being exposed to this world, and many are becoming victims also.

TEACHING YOUR CHILDREN

Children need training from their parents. They need to know that pornography is not only immoral, but it also distorts God's design for love, intimacy, and human dignity. Porn objectifies women and profanes the sanctity of sexual relations designed by our Creator within the confines of marriage. It feeds carnal lust which undermines God's plan for sexual intimacy in marriage.

Pornography desensitizes, distorts, and disorders a person's perspective of sex, creating unrealistic expectations for actual sexual intimacy in marriage. It ruins the God-given blessing intended.

Porn is stealing something that doesn't belong to the consumer. Porn peddlers are selling something that doesn't belong to them. Porn models and performers are giving something that God has not authorized them to give.

Let's get to the heart of the problem. What are consumers of porn looking for? What is driving them? Why do they start, and why do they stay? At what point, does it become bondage to sin?

When and why does it become an addiction? How does it degrade relationships? How does it disrupt a person's physical wellbeing? What are the effects on a person's mental health? There are answers to all of these questions. As parents, we want to know how to help our children navigate through this minefield and walk in freedom.

First things first—clothing. In the beginning, before sin, Adam, and Eve "were both naked, the man and his wife, and were not ashamed" (Genesis 2:25). This reminds us of the innocence that existed before sin. Shame exists with a consciousness of sin and from disordered thoughts or actions. When Adam and Eve sinned, everything began to change even before God pronounces judgement. "Then the eyes of both of them were opened, and they knew that they were naked; and they sewed fig leaves together and made themselves coverings." (Genesis 3:7). They rightly felt ashamed of their nakedness, and they made makeshift coverings to clothe themselves.

Afterwards, God covered them with the skins of animals. He performed the first animal sacrifice: Innocent animals were killed and skinned by God to provide the clothing. This is our first glimpse of atonement which ultimately points to the atoning blood of Jesus Christ for our sins. Let's not miss the point that from the time that Adam and Eve sinned, nakedness became shameful. They covered themselves, and God covered them more thoroughly. Mankind's need for clothing becomes part of a Biblical worldview 101 lesson. When God gave the Law through Moses, He clarified that nakedness, in a sexual context, doesn't belong to just anyone: it only belongs between a husband and wife. Any other sexualized nakedness is sin—sin to be naked and sin to see naked. If that sounds old fashioned, it is as old as Eden.

Boys especially and girls also can become curious at a young age to know how the opposite sex is different. Their curiosity may or may not begin with sexual thoughts, but it often ends there. Remember, innocence is gone in the human race, and though young children have a period of time where they are oblivious to nakedness, they don't remain in that ignorance. The initial motivation of curiosity is often a gateway to new sexually driven motivations to look at porn.

The next phase of a child looking for porn comes from the awareness that seeing someone else's nakedness of the opposite sex is not appropriate or allowed by God and by God fearing adults. It becomes sexual curiosity and a sexual thrill to see what has been appropriately hidden from view. They want to see what they are not allowed to see. This is temptation 101. A desire, a thrill, or a craving does not mean something is okay because there is an internal urge. They are not seeing nudity only, but sexual acts, increasingly darker and manifesting a desensitized and depraved perspective. Porn is not the sex ed your children need; instead, it is the kind that twists God's design for sex out of all proportion. The word perverted means something that is twisted that should be straight.

Children today are not always being taught the truth about their sexual nature. Their God-given sexual nature is intended to find purpose and meaning in a covenant of marriage and is part of a package deal. Marriage is not just about sex but faithful companionship, security, provision, and when possible, the procreation of children. This sexual nature is like fire that must be handled properly and kept in its proper place; otherwise, it can wreak havoc and destroy instead of being useful in the right context.

God gave His law through Moses to govern His people, to make sure they knew right from wrong. This external law of the Old Covenant is necessary until a transformation of the heart through the New Covenant. Through the redemption of Jesus and the internal work of His Holy Spirit, lives can be transformed and the external law written on the heart so that we not only understand what is right and wrong but desire to do what is right and forsake what is wrong. Make no mistake, your children need the law until their hearts are transformed.

> But before faith came, we were kept under guard by the law, kept for the faith which would afterward be revealed. Therefore, the law was our tutor to bring us to Christ, that we might be justified by faith. But after faith has come, we are no longer under a tutor.—Galatians 3:23-25

Did I mention that I'm a fulltime pastor of a church? I've been pastoring for over twenty years. It has been all too common to counsel parents whose children have been exposed to porn. Almost two decades ago I remember sitting with a parent who discovered their eight-year-old son sneaking to a computer in the middle of the night to view porn. The boy's behavior was no longer mere curiosity. This young boy was old enough to get caught in the web of lust. This example is just one of many anecdotal stories that I have encountered as a pastor caring for a flock.

The Bible says in 1 Corinthians 10:13, "No temptation has overtaken you except such as is common to man; but God is faithful, who will not allow you to be tempted beyond what you are able, but with the temptation will also make the way of escape, that you may be able to bear it." We must instruct our children about resisting temptation and the sin of pornography. They need to know from us and from God's law that pornography is sinful and shameful. Seemingly, everyone else in today's culture is attempting to convince kids that seeing nudity is okay.

THE BRAIN AND PORNOGRAPHY

Morality matters, and pornography is a moral issue. It is also a child development issue. One of the consequences from porn exposure in children is how it effects the reward system of the brain that triggers dopamine. The relationship between porn use and dopamine is documented through scientific studies.

What is dopamine? It is a neurotransmitter or, in common language, a chemical messenger that our bodies use to send signals in the brain. What kind of signals? A sense of pleasure for one thing, but dopamine also affects the cycle of motivation, rewards, and reinforced behaviors. Pornography triggers a surge of dopamine in the brain in a similar way as drugs, gambling, and video games and reinforces the behavior through the resulting thoughts like, "That made me feel good—I should do it again." When the activity is repeated, it establishes a cycle that begins with a trigger, such as boredom, lustful thoughts, depression, or curiosity. These feelings lead to the desire to view porn again. The act of viewing porn leads to the reward in the brain through another dopamine release. The cycle is complete, and the behavior is reinforced. This cycle eventually establishes a disordered pattern of habituation or even addiction.

Mounting problems stem from the design of the brain to try to adjust to the abnormal levels of dopamine. The body's attempt to normalize can lessen the previous good feelings from porn, gambling, drugs, or video games. It is referred to as the increase of tolerance, which results in a lesser high from the dopamine hit. This disappointing decrease often leads to an increase in activity and the intensity of the activity. For the drug user, it means more frequent use of drugs and eventually harder drugs. Guess what? It's the same for porn: more frequent use and eventually harder porn.

If this cycle continues, it begins to rewire the brain, but not in a good way. The other side of this problem is the lessening of good and natural rewards through healthy relationships, hard work and achievement, and other activities that naturally trigger dopamine. But they trigger a normal or ordered level of dopamine that is much less than porn. They are no longer as rewarding as they once were in comparison with porn.

Neuroscience has discovered that the brain's wiring can change. It's called neuroplasticity, and it works by laying down new pathways from frequent use or by the diminishing of old pathways no longer in use. Think of a field with tall grass. If you walk through the middle of that field once, you might discern a faint path afterwards. If let alone for a day or two, no one would know anyone had trekked across it unless they were a highly trained tracker. However, if you walk across the field again the next day, follow your faint tracks, a new trail will start to form. Continue this day after day and you will establish a well-worn path to follow. It's not as if you couldn't start a new path, but the likelihood and convenience of your established path makes it unlikely that you will change course, especially when we consider why you cut across the field as you did in the first place. Why? Because there was an initial temptation that at the other end of that field would be a reward, and there was a reward, but not a moral reward.

This process of neuroplasticity is more pronounced in a young person, for they are still in a developmental stage of life. Brain plasticity continues from the cradle to the grave, but it is dramatically heightened in childhood and youth. Long-term effects from dopamine dysregulation are also found in children. Overstimulation eventually dulls the normal dopamine mechanism, leading to emotional numbness, depression, and apathy. The problem is recognized by some experts as "porn-induced anhedonia." Anhedonia means the inability to feel pleasure or joy from normal experiences that usually produce joy and pleasure in humanity. It is also known to affect a person's motivation to pursue these normal human experiences.

Thankfully, much of this can be reversed if the cycle of dysregulation is stopped and normal activities are resumed. It takes time, but the brain can reset, especially when parents are present to guide the process and help rebuild the right paths. This process is sometimes referred to as a dopamine detox, a reboot, or a reset.

PHYSICAL DEBILITATION

We are "fearfully and wonderfully made" (Ps. 139:14) by our all-knowing and all-powerful Creator. We have a body, a mind, emotions, and a spirit, all working together to make us a complete person. When any one of these elements of humanity are disordered, it also affects the others. Here's an example, when you are watching an emotionally dramatic scene in a movie, it can trigger a physical response of tears. Those tears welling up in your eyes and running down your cheeks are physical tears. They are real and were initiated through a dramatic scene and moving music. The opposite can also happen. You can be physically sick with flu, or suffering pain from an injury, and your emotional state is affected negatively. Numerable anecdotes demonstrate this point.

One example related to ongoing porn use is the increasing problem of erectile dysfunction in young men. Porn negatively affects the body as well as the mind, the heart, and the spirit.

ENDNOTES

1   Michael B. Robb and Supreet Mann, "Teens and Pornography," 2023, https://www.commonsensemedia.org/sites/default/files/research/report/2022-teens-and-pornography-final-web.pdf.

CHAPTER 15

THE DARK SIDE OF SCREEN TIME: GIRLS' BODY IMAGE

He created them male and female, and blessed them and called them Mankind in the day they were created.

—Genesis 5:2

I believe that just as the enemy of our soul, Satan, uses pornography to cripple and bind men, he uses the body image issue to destroy women.

—Heather Creekmore

You don't have to be an expert or consult scientific research to know there are major differences between males and females. We can observe these differences without any special accreditation. Our Creator not only designed the two genders with different reproductive biological traits, but there are also differences in neurological wiring in the brain, emotional tendencies, motivations, hormones, and behaviors. All of these differences are helpful to explain why boys in general struggle more than girls with pornography, and girls in general struggle more than boys with body image. There are always exceptions, but these differences are confirmed by scientific research and studies. Boys, more often than girls, seek out pornography, view it at a younger age, and are more compulsive consumers of porn than girls.

I've touched on the issue of pornography in the previous chapter. Now, we need to look at the dark side of screen time causing problems with girls about body image. Screen driven distortions about body image can result in eating disorders, anxiety, depression, suicidal ideation, self-harm, and suicide. Girls are continually bombarded with messages in social media that their value as a person is defined by being beautiful, thin, and sexually attractive. They are manipulated to believe the lie that they must compete with porn. This pervasive messaging is reinforced in TV, commercial advertisements, movies, and music videos. These various forms of media prominently feature sexualized female bodies with the intent of pleasing sexually charged males. When girls are exposed to porn, they sometimes perceive it as their competition, what they have to level up to for attention.

Just as the issue of porn has underlying desires that have been distorted, girls have genuine underlying desires that are being twisted. Girls have a deep need to be loved, desired, accepted, and affirmed. Ultimately, their deepest needs are not fulfilled through a boyfriend, a future husband, or male attention in general, but through a right relationship with God through their Savior, Jesus Christ. They need help understanding that having the attention of a man is good when it is in the right context, at the right time of life, and is safe within the boundaries set by God. To be genuinely loved is not dependent on a socially warped perspective of beauty.

A girl's deepest needs can be realized only through her identity in Christ. I don't say this to be cliché or preachy or to offer a cheesy Christian platitude, but rather as a true north direction for our daughters. The answer to the problem is not found in achieving body positivity over a negative body image. Instead, it is about understanding that a focus on the body, positive or negative, misses the mark for what your daughter truly needs, whether she knows it or not.

> The opposite of body hatred isn't body love. They are two sides of the same pride problem. If we want to experience true body freedom, having more body pride will never be the way out. Spending more time esteeming ourselves cannot be the best answer.[1]—Heather Creekmore

Over two decades, I have been speaking about the danger of worshipping the idols of entertainment. We don't think of ourselves as an idolatrous culture because we don't know anyone that actually bows down and offers sacrifices to stone or wood statues. Our idols are more sophisticated than carved figures: they are living and breathing musicians, actors, athletes, and fame in general, no matter how fame was gained. Sometimes, they don't even have to be living anymore. But the greatest idol of our time has become "self." The idolization of oneself in an effort to become part of the modern pantheon of gods who are worshipped by others.

Humans were created by God as worshippers. We are wired to worship our Creator. Sin ruined that. In the book of Romans, the apostle Paul tells us what happens when people turn their back on God. They don't cease to be worshippers; their worship is diverted to the creature instead of their Creator.

> Therefore God also gave them up to uncleanness, in the lusts of their hearts, to dishonor their bodies among themselves, who exchanged the truth of God for the lie,

and worshiped and served the creature rather than the Creator, who is blessed forever. Amen.—Romans 1:24-25

Devotion, attention, fixation, and obsession would be appropriate words to describe a worshipper of the one true God. They are dangerous words when they describe anything else. Yes, a girl's body image obsession applies. So does a boy's obsession with pornography. I could make a lengthy list of idolatrous obsessions, but hopefully you get the point. Your role as a Christian parent is not to convince your daughter to idolize beauty in order to fix her obsession with a negative body image. Your role is to point her to Christ to find real meaning, real identity, real purpose, and peace with God's sovereignty in her life.

In the din of today's toxic messaging to girls, the adults in the room are forgetting to pass along age old wisdom and truth to counter the lies. It can help to be truthful with our daughters that not everyone is given the same external traits that culture deems more beautiful. I love the following quote from Heather Creekmore in her book *Compared to Who? A Proven Path to Improve Your Body Image.*

> The Bible doesn't shy away from telling us some women were considered beautiful (Rachel) while others weren't (Leah) (Gen.29:17). I never understood how God could make that distinction between these two sisters. How could he point out that one woman radiated hotness while the other looked better with a veil on? Didn't he know that he made all women beautiful? Where was the footnote in my Bible that said Leah had dim eyes but great thighs? And then I realized something. It's okay for God to point out that some women have great physi-

cal beauty and others don't because he knows the truth about beauty. The beauty God designed and the idol of beauty worshipped by our culture are not one and the same.[2]

Girls who may not be considered beautiful by our culture's superficial standards need to know that their value and attractiveness are not dependent on mere external traits. And if they could magically change how they looked, it would not resolve the root problem of making an idol out of beauty.

> Beauty neither solves our problems nor gives us what we hope.[3]—Heather Creekmore

The beauty standards set by entertainment, advertising, and social media are not what will secure a satisfying and lasting life. The external beauty that is admired by the masses can be a stumbling block if beauty is idolized and true value defined by the Creator is spurned or ignored. God has not been silent on the subject. Ponder what the Creator says.

> Charm is deceptive, and beauty is fleeting; but a woman who fears the LORD is to be praised.—Proverbs 31:30 (NIV)

> Like a gold ring in a pig's snout is a beautiful woman who shows no discretion.—Proverbs 11:22 (NIV)

When is the last time you had a conversation in your home about the fear of the Lord? I made the case in my book *Media Choices: Convictions or Compromise?* that the best internet filter is the fear of the Lord. It is also an applicable subject for our daughters and their battle with charm and beauty.

If you struggle with comprehending how and why the Bible makes so many references to the fear of the Lord, don't worry, you're not alone. As a pastor, I have encountered many people in my own congregation that struggle with it. I don't want to shift the subject right now away from girl's body image issues, but if you want to dive deeper you can find an article on the subject at MediaTalk101.com or read the chapter The Best Internet Filter in my book *Media Choices: Convictions or Compromise?* For now, it can help to know that God says, "A woman who fears the Lord is to be praised." He places a higher value on this over charm and beauty.

We need to remind our daughters that being human is not just about having a body; we also have souls. The prevailing worldview attempts to create a division and keep these two parts separate. How can we help our daughters when they think life would be better if they were more attractive? Where are they getting their definition of what it means to be attractive? Do they understand that the biggest battle they are facing is not their outward appearance but an internal struggle. The real war they are facing is found in the heart, the soul, and the mind. God's word speaks to the whole person. In fact, Jesus taught that the greatest commandment is to love God with all your heart, soul, mind, and strength.

God's Word doesn't teach us that we must love ourselves. In fact, it says if we want to follow Jesus, we must deny ourselves, take up a cross and follow Him. This compounding problem of body negativity among girls today is a problem of self-focus. Our girls are bombarded with messages from entertainment to love themselves and follow their hearts. It is essentially a call to worship the creation rather than the Creator. Worshipping our own body or someone else's is idolatry. Our bodies are a gift from God to be used to worship Him.

Our daughters and granddaughters exist in a world steeped in toxic comparisons. Most of the comparison is upward. I wrote about the meaning of upward comparison in the chapter about social media. Others look better, get more attention, and are more popular. But these standards do not define meaningful and fulfilling life. Toxic comparison does not define a girl's worth. Limiting screen time helps slow the stream of toxic content. Going on a media fast can stop the stream for a time and allow for a reset.

Screentime behavior is often a symptom of a deeper issue, a heart issue. At the same time, the negative influence that often comes from screentime is problematic. It continues to plant the wrong seeds and cultivate the wrong ideas.

> Whoever sows to please their flesh, from the flesh will reap destruction; whoever sows to please the Spirit, from the Spirit will reap eternal life.—Galatians 6:8 (NIV)

It's time to sow to please the Spirit not the flesh. Let's teach our daughters about the beauty that radiates from a girl who is at peace with God, a girl who exudes real joy, and a girl who loves Jesus. These may not be the traits a godless young man is looking for in a young woman, but in that case, he's not the kind of guy she should want attention from anyway. The following Bible verse gives us some insight into what our Creator thinks about true beauty:

> Your adornment must not be merely the external—braiding the hair, wearing gold jewelry, or putting on apparel; but it should be the hidden person of the heart, with the

imperishable quality of a gentle and quiet spirit, which is precious in the sight of God.—1 Peter 3:3-4 (NASB)

There is a true beauty that transcends mere physical beauty. Better yet, this kind of beauty is achievable, and it is within reach for our daughters and granddaughters. It is important to teach your children about having the right values in life. A value is something you believe to have greater worth than something else and should be prioritized over other things. Jesus used the word treasure. What do you treasure?

Do not lay up for yourselves treasures on earth, where moth and rust destroy and where thieves break in and steal; but lay up for yourselves treasures in heaven, where neither moth nor rust destroys and where thieves do not break in and steal. For where your treasure is, there your heart will be also.—Matthew 6:19-21

Here's the truth, outward beauty fades. The thieves of aging break in and rob everyone in time. Outward beauty will be taken away; it is temporary at best. But the true beauty that can be attained through Jesus is eternal. Let's help our girls to know that there is better treasure in heaven than on earth, but they must learn to lay up that treasure now.

Girls' body image is a daunting subject and to do it justice requires a book of its own, so I heartily recommend the resources available from Heather Creekmore. There are a couple more issues I would like to touch on in this section on the dark side of screen time.

As we venture a little deeper, don't lose heart. There's light at the end of this tunnel. I close this chapter with one final but pertinent quote from Heather.

> Media is the chain that binds us to our body image battle. Take action and free yourself from its captivity.[4]

ENDNOTES

1   Heather Creekmore, Compared to Who?: A Proven Path to Improve Your Body Image (Abilene Christian University Press, 2017).

2   Ibid.

3   Ibid.

4   Ibid.

CHAPTER 16

THE DARK SIDE OF SCREEN TIME: USER-GENERATED CONTENT, SEXTORTION, PREDATORS, AND ACTION STEPS

DIY PORN: USER GENERATED CONTENT

One of the most common forms of user generated porn is through sexting—sending and receiving explicit messages and nude pictures through phones. This risky behavior is becoming more prevalent among teens. What may have started with a desire for attention or pressure from a boyfriend or girlfriend can morph into blackmail, extortion, revenge sharing, bullying, social shaming, and sometimes lead to despair and suicide. According to research published in Journal of Adolescent Health[1], 19.3% of teenagers have sent a sext message, 34.8% have received a sext message, and 14.5% have forwarded a sext message.

As a parent, you may find it daunting to have a conversation about sexting. If your middle or high schooler doesn't have access to a smartphone, then you may be able to delay this subject, and it would be a better plan overall for you to delay access to smartphones as long as reasonable. However, if you have given your child a phone then you are also making a choice that requires you to have these kinds of discussions.

What might that conversation sound like? First, it would be good to define and explain what sexting is. Your children should be educated so they can identify the problem clearly if they are solicited for a photo or video or if they receive an unsolicited photo or video. They also need to know that it's not just text messages but can also be problematic in a variety of apps. Next, help your child understand that they should bring any problems to your attention as soon as possible without fear of being in trouble. The first priority is making sure there is an open channel of communication and a safe zone they can be confident about. Let them know you won't blame, shame, or judge them if they feel that they are trapped, pressured, or have already crossed a line. You want to be a refuge.

It's also helpful to talk about the consequences of sharing sexual images. Besides the moral inappropriateness, once the image leaves a device, there is no guarantee it remains with the recipient. Other teens involved are already demonstrating their lack of wisdom and maturity so it shouldn't be surprising when the images are then used against the person who originally took and sent the picture or video. The practice of peddling these images or using them for sextortion is certainly cruel, and it is happening at alarming rates. This has led to haunting regret, painful shame, and debilitating anxiety. There are also possible legal ramifications in many states for having nude images of anyone under eighteen years old.

Spiritually, it's a violation of God's order and a sin against one's own body and soul. If intentionally receiving these kinds of texts, it is a sin against others and against God.

As you engage your children in conversations about phone and internet safety, it can also be an occasion to talk with your kids about the problems of peer pressure and the longing to be liked and affirmed. True friendship protects. Real love does not demand from others what is wrong for them to give, even if it is socially acceptable behavior among peers. What is truly acceptable is determined by a loving God, not immature teens with underdeveloped brains and calloused hearts. Let your child know that it is a heroic effort to resist this kind of peer pressure. Be sure to keep the heartstrings tied to your children and affirm what is right. Their body belongs first and foremost to God, and nudity does not belong to anyone other than a future spouse. They will not find value by devaluing themselves to fuel the perversions and sexual deviancies of others.

One easy hack I learned about is to teach your kids to blame you for saying no if they are ever pressured by others to share nude pictures or videos. They can boldly say to the solicitor that there's no way because Dad and Mom regularly check the phone, and they would have their phone taken away and be grounded for life. Of course, you should be checking their phone regardless. Another helpful hint is to block any app that allows disappearing messages, such as Snapchat and other similar apps. It's not uncommon for perpetrators to convince someone to send a photo or video using one of these apps with the false promise that it can't be stored. There's always a work around, and those workarounds are known and being used. It's not certain that the image or video will disappear forever.

Lastly, you need to talk to your kids about the growing practice of sextortion. If you don't know what that is, I'll address it later in this chapter. I've given you plenty of talking points to help get you started. When should you start? Before you decide to put a smartphone in your children's hands. If they are attending public school or are online for homeschool, you need to start the conversation whenever you decide you're going to trust them online or with a smartphone without your constant watchfulness. Don't forget that there are viable alternatives to smartphones. If needed, revisit the chapter My Children as Guinea Pigs.

SG-CSAM

Unfortunately, things can get even darker. The shortened description of SG-CSAM stands for self-generated child sexual abuse material, (CSAM is considered child pornography). This material is being circulated online and being consumed by abusers. According to a report called Youth Perspectives on Online Safety, 2023 showed that "1 in 7 minors have shared their own SG-CSAM" and "Roughly 1 in 8 minors know a friend who has received money or gifts in exchange for SG-CSAM."

These images and videos are sometimes the result of minors being groomed, coerced, and exploited online. Other times, they are from teens sexting each other, but this material is often forwarded to others. According to Thorn's report "nearly 1 in 3 teens say they have seen non-consensually shared nudes."[2] Some teen girls are now archiving material to release on sites, such as OnlyFans once they turn eighteen in hope of financial profit.

SEXTORTION

A newer and deeply disturbing threat is known as sextortion. It is the act of coercing someone into sending explicit photos through deceit, manipulation, or threats and then leveraging the material using threats of exposure to get the person to do something else—to extort the victim for money or more sexual content or coercing a victim to remain in a relationship.

Research by Thorn conducted in partnership with the National Center for Missing & Exploited Children (NCMEC) reported[3],

"Sextortion, and particularly financial sextortion, continues to be a major and ongoing threat, with an average of 812 reports of sextortion per week to NCMEC in the last year of data analyzed, and with reason to expect that the vast majority of those reports are financial sextortion." They also reported, "Perpetrators leverage tactics to intentionally fan a victim's worry about the life-changing impacts of their nudes being shared—often repeating claims that it will 'ruin their life.'"

Between 3.5% and 5% of people are believed to have experienced sextortion before reaching adulthood.[4]

ONLINE PREDATORS IN DISGUISE

Online predators don't showcase themselves as monsters. If they did, they might scare children off. Instead, they are disguised as other kids in a chat while playing an online game or a friendly and sympathetic person in a DM. For a teen boy, they may be disguised as a sexy young girl, or for teen girls a cute young guy who is in love with them. The victims are not imagining an overweight man in his forties who is a sexual pervert with dozens of schemes or a foreign actor from Nigeria looking for financial gain or someone working for a notorious criminal gang like the 764 network.

Every app is a potential entry point into your home. You wouldn't hand over the keys to your front door to strangers or invite pedophiles to have private communication with your kids in their rooms. Yet these very things are happening through online encounters with predators.

There are an estimated 500,000 online predators active each day. Children between the ages of 12 and 15 are especially susceptible to be groomed or manipulated by adults they meet online. According to the F.B.I., over 50 percent of the victims of online sexual exploitation are between the ages of 12 and 15. An estimated 89 percent of sexual advances directed at children occur in Internet chatrooms or through instant messaging.[5]—Child Crime Prevention & Safety Center

ENOUGH IS ENOUGH

I don't know about you, but I'm weary from addressing the dark side of screen time, it drains me, and I don't like it at all. As parents, we cannot bury our heads in the sand and hope that the really dark stuff will mysteriously go away. There are more topics that are also part of the dark side of screen time, like cyberbullying, online sexual encounters, AI driven sextortion, dark criminal networks and more. If you want to learn more, please educate yourself but for now, my own soul is taxed from writing this section and I'm guessing that you may also be drained from reading it. I want to go back to the beginning and remind you of the action plan I laid out for your family.

My call to action is to implement a comprehensive family plan to keep your kids safe using the acronym **GRACE**: G̲uardrails, R̲ules, A̲wareness, C̲onversations, and E̲scape routes.

G̲uardrails are the technology options available to you for monitoring and blocking content. The guardrails you put in place also includes limiting access to technology until an appropriate age. Don't skip over Appendix 1 at the end of this book.

R̲ules stands for household rules. They are decided by you, the parents. They are for your children's safety and wellbeing, not because you want to make life more difficult for them or for you. Good rules exist for good reasons.

AWARENESS is teaching your children about *why* you have guardrails and rules. Help them to understand your reasoning based on your love for them and their best interests at heart.

CONVERSATIONS are ongoing discussions. Make screen time a regular subject of discussion in your family and have age-appropriate talks about the common traps of the dark side.

Lastly, have predetermined **ESCAPE ROUTES**. If the above safety measures fail or are neglected, and your child finds themselves in online trouble, they need to know without question that it is safe to come to you without fear.

One more quick review of the acronym **GRACE**: **G**UARDRAILS, **R**ULES, **A**WARENESS, **C**ONVERSATIONS, and **E**SCAPE ROUTES. The acronym is a helpful reminder that this is about love, not law.

ENDNOTES

1. Camille Mori et al., "Are Youth Sexting Rates Still on the Rise? A Meta-analytic Update," Journal of Adolescent Health 70, no. 4 (December 13, 2021): 531–39, https://doi.org/10.1016/j.jadohealth.2021.10.026.

2. Thorn, "Thorn Research: Understanding Sexually Explicit Images, Self-produced by Children," Thorn, February 20, 2024, https://www.thorn.org/blog/thorn-research-understanding-sexually-explicit-images-self-produced-by-children/.

3. Thorn and National Center for Missing and Exploited Children (NCMEC). (2024). Trends in Financial Sextortion: An investigation of sextortion reports in NCMEC CyberTipline data.

4. Patchin, Justin W. and S. Hinduja. "Sextortion Among Adolescents: Results From a National Survey of U.S. Youth." Sexual Abuse: A Journal of Research and Treatment 32 (2020): 30 - 54.; Finkelhor, David, Heather A. Turner and Deirdre Colburn. "Prevalence of Online Sexual Offenses Against Children in the US." JAMA Network Open 5 (2022)

5. "Children and Grooming / Online Predators," Child Crime Prevention & Safety Center, n.d., https://childsafety.losangelescriminallawyer.pro/children-and-grooming-online-predators.html.

CHAPTER 17

BATTLING BOREDOM

Boredom is not a boring subject. If you consult the original Webster's 1828 dictionary and look up the word *boredom,* it's not there. If you look up *bored,* you'll read the following, "Perforated by an auger or other turning instrument; made hollow."

It seems that boredom is something new in our culture. In an article in The New York Times, Richard Friedman writes,

> The very concept of boredom seems to be a modern invention …the word boredom did not enter the lexicon until the mid-19th century. Before that, tedium was an expected part of life. It was only with the rise of consumer culture in the 20th century that people were promised nearly continuous excitement; boredom was the inevitable consequence of such unrealistic expectations.

Boredom is incubated in a culture with lots of time for leisure. This cultural trend has emerged gradually since the Industrial Revolution when it became more common for people to work away from home instead of running a farm or a family business. Before the Industrial Revolution, kids often went to school until 6th or 8th grade and then most of them pitched in to work in the family business.

I realize that we are not living in the era of *Little House on the Prairie*.[1] Times have changed drastically when it comes to the normative experience of children growing up in today's digital age versus growing up in a non-electric world of a child on a farm with a multitude of chores and no shortage of necessary work to be done as a family. The kids in *Little House on the Prairie* didn't get bored; they simply dealt with tedium in life, which wasn't a terrible thing.

Tedium or things that are tedious are not the same thing as boredom. Boredom is an emotional state when you are doing nothing and are unmotivated to do something. One dictionary defines boredom as "the state of feeling bored."[2]

Tedium on the other hand is understood only in the context of doing something. It is doing something that is tiresome or keeping occupied with a task that is repetitive. It is something that takes time and is not exciting or entertaining. Tedium has actual value, but boredom has none. Another word in the Bible that describes tedium is *toil*.

In Ecclesiastes 5:18, King Solomon writes, "Here is what I have seen: It is good and fitting for one to eat and drink, and to enjoy the good of all his labor in which he toils under the sun all the days of his life which God gives him; for it is his heritage."

King Solomon connects labor with toil, which is not entertaining, but it is essential to a purposeful and meaningful life. Time for a reality check: real life, even a heroic life, is full of tedium.

The day-to-day stuff of real life takes hard work, perseverance, and choosing to do hard tasks. A meaningful life is not found by merely taking the path of least resistance. No special talent or skill is needed to zone out in front of a screen to be entertained.

We are all easily enamored with heroic stories compressed into an action packed ninety-minute feature film. Those compelling stories, especially the ones based on real life events, if played out for you in real time, would be tedious and boring! The exciting feature film or the multi-season, episodic TV shows do not reflect the reality of day-to-day life. Not even reality shows reflect the reality of day-to-day life. They are often scripted and edited to entertain.

If we are committed to finding balance and regaining focus, they cannot be found by trying to imitate a world that no longer exists without electricity and other modern technologies. Neither will it be found through heedless enthusiasm that neglects to consider the importance of limitations and self-control.

The answer to the problem of boredom is not more entertainment. Your family is better than that. Your family has more purpose than merely becoming screen zombies when bored. Media use begets more media use, meaning the more time you spend on a screen, the more screen time grows in your limited schedule. Like rabbits, screen time begets its own kind.

Excessive screen time can be a black hole that sucks the purpose out of your family's life. It doesn't satisfy your deepest longing for purpose and meaning. It only allows you to temporarily escape and live vicariously in the moment. In fact, the more time your children spend in front of a screen, the more likely they will be distracted from discovering purpose and meaning in life. Did you know that one of the most effective cures for boredom is purpose?

I have found that many young people don't understand purpose. They can't answer the questions, "What is the purpose of existence?" or "What is the meaning of life?" and specifically, "Why am I here?"

We all ask questions about purpose and meaning because there is an intrinsic sense that there must be some meaning to life. We have a baked in desire to leave some legacy, but how?

Most teens have a basic longing to experience meaningful goals, such as seeing new places, having deep friendships, being successful at work, finding a career, starting their own business, pursuing a hobby, being good at a sport, becoming proficient on a musical instrument, or getting married someday.

Yet if these things bring fulfillment to humanity's need for purpose, then why are there so many broken relationships between friends, relatives, parents, and children? What about all the disappointment and discontentment people experience at work and in their careers? In fact, many people when thinking about purpose think about a career. No matter what your children eventually do in life for work, if they define purpose by a career, they'll likely become disillusioned. Many people don't end up doing what they envisioned themselves doing, or they eventually lose their job and must do something different. Some people get their dream job only to realize it is not so dreamy in real life. Others, through circumstances out of their control, find it impossible or too difficult to pursue their desired career.

Not even wealthy, popular, beautiful movie stars or musicians have gained contentment by attempting to find purpose and meaning in their career. Many live miserable lives, some ending in suicide or drug overdoses, or they leave a wake behind them of broken relationships.

WHAT IS OUR PURPOSE?

Many young people ponder the question, "What is the purpose of my existence?" If they don't understand their purpose, the negative impact in their lives extends beyond how they choose to spend their time when they are bored.

Using a few inanimate objects may help when trying to understand purpose. The main purpose of a car is to provide transportation. You can do other things with a car or in a car, but it has a primary purpose. The purpose of an office stapler is to attach a small stack of papers together quickly. The main purpose of a fork is to help you eat your food, especially food that can be more easily managed with a fork versus a spoon.

These are all easy to identify because they are inanimate objects and are not overly complex. A car is more complex than a fork, but your children are infinitely more complex than any inanimate object. What about your children? What is their purpose, and do they understand it? We are told in Ecclesiastes 3:1, "To everything there is a season, a time for every purpose under heaven." In Psalms 20:4 it says, "May He grant you according to your heart's desire, and fulfill all your purpose."

If your children are going to discover their purpose, they need help finding their answers from God, not from entertainment. God created them with a purpose in mind. He holds the patent and copyright, so to speak, for humanity. He invented us, He made us. He knows more about us than we know about ourselves.

Did you know that someone once asked Jesus about purpose? A man wanted to know what Jesus considered to be the most important instructions God gave in the Bible to mankind. Listen to His answer.

> Jesus said to him, "You shall love the Lord your God with all your heart, with all your soul, and with all your mind. This is the first and great commandment. And the second is like it: You shall love your neighbor as yourself. On these two commandments hang all the Law and the Prophets."—Matthew 22:37-40

Loving God and our neighbor is our greatest priority in life, and building on this foundation will also fill a person's life with the greatest sense of purpose and meaning. Unfortunately, so many young people don't discover this soon enough, or they don't believe it. They don't believe prioritizing love for God with all of their heart will be rewarding and give them a sense of purpose and meaning in life. They need your help to see this truth in God's word.

If they decide that they're going to join the stubborn masses of young people who think they know better and can find purpose and meaning in life apart from God, they will not only be mistaken, but they will also be disappointed. They will go through life like so many others looking, searching, but never finding what is missing. They will try to find purpose in a career, a hobby, a sport, a relationship with someone, popularity, or having wealth. It is precarious when they wrongly believe their purpose is dependent on something they can lose.

Jesus answered the question. The greatest commandment from God is to love Him with all your heart, soul, mind, and strength. No amount of searching will help you discover anything more important in life.

Your children are designed and created by God for a purpose. That purpose begins with their relationship with God: To acknowledge Him as their Creator and to be reconciled to Him through Jesus.

Ecclesiastes 3:1 says, "To everything there is a season, A time for every purpose under heaven." It seems that there is more than just one purpose in this world. Yet, there's one overarching purpose for our existence, and when that purpose is not prioritized, all other ancillary purposes are like trying to build a house on the sand. It's not stable and can't weather the storms of life.

We are told in 2 Timothy 1:9 that God, "Saved us and called us with a holy calling, not according to our works, but according to His own purpose and grace which was given to us in Christ Jesus before time began." There is a tug-of-war between our own ideas of purpose and God's truth about our purpose. One of the problems is our focus on *self*.

Self is the focal point in our culture for finding purpose. Self is in the way. It's one of the greatest diversions from real purpose and meaning.

In Matthew 16:24-26, Jesus said to His disciples, "If anyone desires to come after Me, let him deny himself, and take up his cross, and follow Me. For whoever desires to save his life will lose it." This command includes our pursuit of purpose and meaning in life. You cannot find life by defining your own purpose. Jesus continued by teaching, "But whoever loses his life for My sake will find it. For what profit is it to a man if he gains the whole world and loses his own soul? Or what will a man give in exchange for his soul?"

Another life changing truth about purpose is found in Ephesians 2:10, which says, "For we are His workmanship, created in Christ Jesus for good works, which God prepared beforehand that we should walk in them." The word "workmanship" in the Greek is *poiema*. It is where we get our word for poem. But it has a broader meaning than poetry. According to Greek language scholar Spiros Zodhiates, *poiema* means, "Something made, a work, workpiece, workmanship."[3]

God has crafted your children by His infinite power and skill with a purpose. Here we are told that there are good works which God has prepared for them to live out. They have a destiny with God. Their unique gifts, talents, skills, personality, and circumstances in their lives belong to God and are to be used for His specific purposes that He has for them.

If they've been told that it is up to them to define or discover something unique to have purpose and meaning, they've been misled. I know because I bought into that lie when I was a teen.

Growing up, I had the instinct that my life had a purpose. My bigger question was about the nature of that purpose. Who or what defined my purpose? As a typical child of the eighties, I grew up with a steady diet of popular television, movies, and music. Some common themes in children's movies produced by Disney and others were believe in yourself or follow your heart and follow your dreams.

These were not presented as classes for worldview instruction with tests or reports to turn in and be graded on. Nevertheless, they were teaching me and the majority of my generation a philosophy about purpose which centered on self. We were taught to focus on self-motivated attitudes and actions. All I needed to do was follow my heart, and I would experience my instinctive purpose in life or at least find that purpose. This ideology was problematic because my heart was a mixed bag of ideas and actions. I had good ideas and bad ideas that I acted on or didn't act on. That behavior seemed to be the case with others around me also. It seemed to fit the early description of mankind given by God in Genesis:

> Then the LORD saw that the wickedness of man was great in the earth, and that every intent of the thoughts of his heart was only evil continually. And the LORD was

sorry that He had made man on the earth, and He was grieved in His heart.—Genesis 6:5-6

A couple of chapters later in Genesis 8:21 God says, "The imagination of man's heart is evil from his youth." Not all my thoughts were evil, only some of them. They were in conflict with the good ideas that were being instilled in me by my parents, pastors, and Sunday school teachers. It was a tension which affected my understanding of purpose.

I did try to live out the philosophy of pop culture even if I did so unconsciously. I set my heart on certain things and followed my heart, but I was continually disappointed. I wanted to be in the popular crowd, but I was unpopular. I wanted the cute girl in class to notice me and like me, but she didn't. The boys and girls who were at least friendly toward me encountered an awkward, insecure boy.

In time, I began to recognize and reflect on the many variables out of my control. My upbringing, my home environment, my DNA. I had to live with my unique abilities as well as my inabilities. Like everyone else, I had my own personality quirks for good and for bad. Moreover, many choices were in my control. Unfortunately, I often made bad choices by following my heart. Reality began to settle in: I couldn't be anything I wanted to be. I couldn't do everything I wanted to do. I couldn't trust my heart to follow it. I lived with disappointments and regrets and became depressed. I didn't have any lasting peace or joy in my life. They were fleeting or elusive. Struggling with depression led to more bad decisions and a downward spiral into skepticism about the purpose and meaning of life. I distrusted that I had a purpose. I distrusted life.

From grade school to middle school and from middle school to high school the tension surrounding purpose and identity gnawed at me like rats who continually chew on things to wear down their ever-growing teeth. I was miserable. Obviously, my story didn't end there, Jesus Christ changed everything and gave me purpose in life. Now, let's bring this chapter back to the beginning. I started with the problem of boredom.

Boredom has grown because of the industrial revolution which brought greater prosperity and gave rise to the technological age. The technological age brought about more leisure time, elective time that kids didn't have much of in ages past. Their lives were filled with tedium that kept them occupied with essential responsibilities in life. Today, our children have lots of time on their hands, and maybe they've lacked a sense of purpose. It is ironic that modern technologies have given us more leisure time, and now we need new technologies to provide entertainment to help fill that extra time. Excessive screen time is distracting your children from finding their purpose in life, and it is also a diversion from fulfilling that purpose. Don't allow screen time to be the default response to your children's boredom.

I realize that in the United States we have experienced prosperity and more leisure than many other countries. If you are from a different country, the principle still applies. Your family may have less elective time in your lives but that doesn't change the responsibility you have to manage your time better. But for those in the U.S. we are doubly responsible to manage our time better than we have been.

So how does purpose in life help us battle boredom? When we finally discover that purpose is found in a life devoted to God and serving others, we begin to understand that our time, especially our elective time, should be used carefully. In the next chapter, I will take the next logical step and talk about what it means to redeem the time. Finding purpose is not only a tremendous help for battling boredom, but also, it helps motivate us to use our time wisely.

ENDNOTES

1. A book series by Laura Ingalls Wilder based on her childhood in late 1800's in the United States and published in the early 1900's. A TV adaption in the 1970's and 80's became a popular television series.

2. "Boredom - Definition | Oxford Advanced Learner's Dictionary at OxfordLearnersDictionaries.com," n.d., https://www.oxfordlearnersdictionaries.com/definition/english/boredom.

3. Spiros Zodhiates, The Complete Word Study New Testament: King James version, 2nd ed. (Nelson Bibles, 1992).

CHAPTER 18

TIME MATTERS

Today, mining for bitcoin and other new digital currencies, is a way for some people to create potential wealth, but you must own some powerful computers, be able to pay the electric bill, and be willing to wait a long time before a single coin is created. In a bygone era, you could grab a pickaxe and go prospecting for gold, silver, diamonds, or you could dive for pearls. These were a few of the ways to look for something that had value and potentially add wealth to your life. But there is something just as valuable if not more valuable than tangible or intangible wealth, and that is time.

Time is finite. You can't go mining to add more time to a minute, to an hour, to a day, a month, or a year. There are sixty seconds in a minute for everyone, sixty minutes in an hour, and twenty-four hours in a day for the rich, the poor, the rural, the urban, and around the globe for all cultures, ethnicities, and economies. You can't make a day longer so what does the Bible mean when it says we must redeem the time?

Ephesians 5:15-16 says, "See then that you walk circumspectly, not as fools but as wise, redeeming the time, because the days are evil." Redeem means you are purchasing something back that you lost, sold, or wasted. But we can't create more time or go back in time and rewind the world's clock, so what is this verse referring to?

The NASB translation says it this way, "Therefore be careful how you walk, not as unwise men but as wise, making the most of your time, because the days are evil." So, redeeming the time means we endeavor to make better use of the limited time that we have.

God established time at the very beginning of creation. In Genesis 1:5 we read, "God called the light Day, and the darkness He called Night. So the evening and the morning were the first day." God intends for us to use time wisely. That reason is why Psalm 90:12 says, "So teach us to number our days, that we may gain a heart of wisdom."

It's important to know that a beneficial use of time does not mean neglecting sleep, rest, or even recreation in life. Though I rarely make time for it, I love lying in a hammock on a beautiful day with a cool breeze blowing across me. Lying there is not only refreshing, but I believe it can also be a way to redeem my time, especially if you're a motivated person who tends to work non-stop without proper rest.

Redeeming the time doesn't mean we are like robots in a factory cranking out production 24/7. It does, however, require us to have discernment, to use wisdom on how to organize our day, our week, our year, and so on.

The Bible doesn't specify how much time a person should spend working, versus recreation, versus education, and so on. But it does instruct us to make the most of our time. This ties into our last chapter about purpose in life. Time is tied to purpose, and purpose directs our attitudes and activities for better or worse.

When there is a lack of purpose, time is no longer viewed as a precious commodity. It is no longer something worth redeeming. Time is not valued. When you place no value on time, it is more easily wasted. There is no motivation to buy it back when it has been treated as cheap.

Let's get really practical now and talk about bringing order into our lives and organizing our time wisely in relation to purpose. How often have you said or heard someone say something like, "I'm having trouble juggling all the different things in my life"? I've said it myself, yet it occurred to me that the metaphor of juggling sets us up for failure and discouragement when a ball gets dropped along the way. There are many things in your life that you should always take responsibility for on an ongoing basis: your relationship with God, your family, your vocation, your weekly gathering as believers in church, and your personal well-being.

It may help to rethink the metaphor and consider the concept of a solar system with planets orbiting around the sun at various distances. Many of these important things in life are not going away, and instead of trying to merely juggle them, how about getting them into proper orbits around the Son.

Psalms 8:3-4 says, "When I consider Your heavens, the work of Your fingers, the moon and the stars, which You have ordained, what is man that You are mindful of him, And the son of man that You visit him?" God knows how to keep everything in the universe in order.

Colossians 1:16-17 reminds us that everything in life is held together by Jesus. "For by Him all things were created, both in the heavens and on earth, visible and invisible, whether thrones or dominions or rulers or authorities—all things have been created through Him and for Him. He is before all things, and in Him all things hold together."

The important things in life need to orbit around Christ who is able to keep them in motion. But not all areas of life should have equal attention. Some things need to have shorter orbits, or more dedicated time, and others have longer orbits, or less dedicated time. For instance, Mars takes 687 days to orbit the sun, almost twice the amount of time for the Earth. Jupiter takes a whopping 4,333 days to orbit the sun. Saturn is 10,759 days. Neptune? 60,190 days compared with Mercury's 88-day orbit.

So, what is the planet Mercury in your life? I want to encourage you to have your personal relationship with Jesus be the closest orbit. Your spiritual well-being is going to affect all the other orbits, and if you don't have this orbit right, then the rest are going to struggle, and you will find yourself reverting to juggling life.

If you are married, then your spouse is your Venus, and though the planet Venus has no moons, if you have children, then your Venus will have one or more that will orbit together.

What should orbit next? What is the Earth in your planetary system? Some would say your vocation, but I would suggest involvement in your local church. I'm not saying that because I'm a pastor of a local church but because in Matthew 6:33 Jesus said, "Seek first the kingdom of God and His righteousness, and all these things shall be added to you." The congregation of Christians is the invention of Christ and has been foundational for His kingdom for over two thousand years.

You'll have to determine your Mars, your Jupiter, and your Saturn. The most important point I hope to make is that they all need to orbit around the Son, Jesus Christ.

Stop the juggling in your attempt to keep all the various things in your life in motion. Instead, submit each of them to God and ask for His help and guidance to keep them in the proper orbit, which in this metaphor is about the time you spend, the frequency, the dedication, the consistency, and the priority that you give to important areas of your life. Once you begin modeling this for your children, you can also begin teaching them these helpful lessons.

It is worthwhile to gain the skills to organize your day, your week, your month, and your year. Start by setting priorities and writing them down. Figure out your fixed schedule versus your elective time.

When it comes to entertainment and your use of technology, it often becomes a blackhole in your little solar system that sucks all of your elective time into it and sometimes your non-elective time. What do I mean by elective and non-elective time? Not all your time in life is free to do with as you please. Everyone, including your children, have various responsibilities in your daily and weekly schedules. That time is what I'm referring to as non-elective time. It is set, and you are obliged to be purposeful with that time according to its intended purpose.

Your children's non-elective time includes school, homework, chores at home, sufficient sleep, mealtimes, and so on. Attending church is hopefully part of your non-elective routine. Christians have been meeting together on a weekly basis on Sundays since the first century to commemorate the resurrection of Christ, to worship Him together, to have fellowship with one another, to pray together, and to receive instruction from God's word.

Encourage your children to get involved in your church where they are able. In our church, the worship team, the audio-visual team, the livestream crew, and the set-up crew are almost entirely teens who have made a commitment to get involved in church.

Use elective time to cultivate face-to-face in person relationships. There is also wisdom in helping your children to blend some of these important orbits in their life. For example, a game of ultimate frisbee with Christian friends can cultivate face-to-face friendships, they get some physcial exercise from non-screen activity, and it can be an opportunity for outreach if you invite unsaved guests. They can encourage one another afterwards to keep their focus on Christ, all within the same time frame that they might have been at home with their face in front of a screen.

Our church has a youth worship band that leads worship at the church several times out of the year and at youth worship nights. They use elective time to practice and rehearse, but it also provides a healthy relational time with one another. Their elective time, their free time, is valuable. How will they use it, how will they invest it wisely?

What are some worthwhile goals you can help your children achieve? To achieve these goals, your family will have to manage your time wisely.

They may want to get a part time job or learn to play an instrument. They could build a tiny home (other young people have done it). Or maybe a tiny home is too much for now, so maybe they can start with building a bookshelf for their rooms. What new skill would they like to gain? It's going to take training and practice, and all of this takes time. Maybe they want to write a book? My friend Daniel Schwabauer has a great writing course for teens called The One Year Adventure Novel. Maybe they aspire to shorter form writing like blogposts or maybe produce a podcast. They might be the visual creative kind of person who can make a short film, or a short animation project.

They should be encouraged to cultivate at least one or two deep friendships, but that also takes time. If they already play a sport, maybe they could use more practice or some special training. They need time. How about mentoring someone younger than them, someone who needs help that they could provide?

I know many young people who have started small businesses while in middle school or high school. They can learn a new craft. How about getting that lawnmower working that is sitting in the garage or shed? Or how about the culinary arts? Do they like cooking, baking, or both? There are so many options, I'm just touching the surface with these few suggestions. Help your children make a list of short-term and long-term goals. It's also important to stay physically fit and healthy, so help them factor in time for exercise, good sleep, and a balanced diet.

Regardless of what specifics they pursue with their limited time, some universal pursuits take dedication when it comes to personal spiritual development. These take time but they are essential. Prayer, reading the Bible, and reading other good books should become habits. Harry S. Truman once said, "Not all readers are leaders, but all leaders are readers."

I began this lesson with an illustration about searching for valuables, such as gold or silver. But let's imagine for a moment that money was like time, and everyone who is born was given a lump sum of money just as you have a limited amount of time entrusted to you. Imagine that once you received your lump sum of money at the beginning of your life, you would never be able to gain more as you grew older and became more mature.

Immature children are likely to spend a lot of that money on meaningless things, but as they get older and wiser, they might begin to realize that their account is getting low, and they are not sure how they are going to make it stretch and be used in meaningful and beneficial ways.

Well, thankfully, money is not like time in that way, but time is like time in that way, and hopefully you get the point of why redeeming the time matters. You only have so much in your lifetime, and you cannot create more.

CHAPTER 19

TOOLS OR TOYS?

This generation has access to some of the most powerful digital tools of any generation but what they do with these tools depends on their personal awareness of what's helpful, harmful, or simply a waste of time. Are they able to discern between these and have the discipline to choose what's better and best? Most kids today see these devices as toys. They are the ultimate portal for amusement. I want to encourage you as a parent to help them understand the importance of not just being passive consumers but rather active producers of good.

The smartphone can be a powerful tool if used wisely. In fact, many of today's technologies are not inherently evil, but they are powerful. In the words of Uncle Ben to Peter Parker in *Spider-Man*, "With great power comes great responsibility." Today's technologies are not always the problem. It is often how we use them.

Our problem is not confined to smartphones. Similar concerns arise when considering computers, video game consoles, televisions, and other electronic devices. Growing in media discernment does not mean we have to live life without smartphones and other technologies, but it does mean we need self-control and wisdom to know how to handle these powerful tools carefully.

Are these new technologies under control, or is your family under their spell? This generation is suffering from its love affair with all things tech, and the results manifest in extremes, such as texting and driving deaths, sleep deprivation, inattentiveness to others, the lost practice of reflection and deep thought, and the neglect of Bible reading and prayer, just to name a few.

These digital tools allow us to connect and communicate around the world, but have we lost track of the people in our own house and across the table from us? Just as media can be helpful or harmful, technologies can be blessings or burdens. These two subjects, technology and media, are inevitably jumbled together because they correlate to each other.

The etymology of the word entertainment from Latin means to hold the attention or interest. In that case, I hope this book is entertaining in that original sense of the word. I hope it holds your attention to enable me to teach these helpful truths to your family and that you personally benefit from it. All entertainment intends to hold your attention, but not all entertainment has the same end goal with your attention. Facebook and other social media want to hold your attention so that they can sell your time to advertisers.

The Saturday morning cartoons I watched as a kid were intended to amuse children and, therefore, make their parents happy to own a television and tune into their station to sell advertising and stay in business. The words entertain and amuse are quite different.

The word amuse comes from the root word *muse* which means to think deeply about something. When you put the letter *a* in front of the word *muse* it makes it a negative and literally means *to not think*.

Speaking of definitions, let me add another word, which is *recreation*. I believe there's an appropriate place in our lives for recreation. One dictionary gives the following definitions for recreation: "The refreshment of the mind and body after work, especially by engaging in enjoyable activities" and "an activity that a person takes part in for pleasure or relaxation rather than work."

I love the Webster's 1828 dictionary, which defines recreation as, "Refreshment of the strength and spirits after toil; amusement; diversion " and "relief from toil or pain; amusement in sorrow or distress." There's a need for re-creation of strength and spirits after a time of toil or a diversion from sorrow or distress. Today, many young people and some adults avoid work to amuse themselves through screen time. That's not a true reflection of what recreation is intended to be. When recreation undermines work and is used to escape difficulties in life, it is no longer recreation in its proper sense; it is diversion and amusement, which leads to an imbalanced life. Instead of bringing relief or renewal, it robs a person of living life with purpose. Recreation, when kept in its proper place, has a beneficial purpose in your family's life.

Let's consider some alternate forms of recreation to the default of more screen time. Let me warn you that many ideas will cost you more time, energy, and possibly money than you usually spend with your children. Let's ease into this by pointing you to board games. A board game is interactive. It can foster conversation while playing the game. They are not usually addictive, but they do require more energy than passively watching a screen. I confess that there are times I would rather not play a board game. Plus, the games my kids want to play are not always the games I would prefer to play and vice versa. I'm probably not alone in my apprehension, and I suppose that many parents, like me, would rather take the path of least resistance and zone out in front of the TV with the kids.

There are likely a thousand ideas that you could consider as alternatives to screen time. I'll let you do your own thinking, but I'll share a few personal decisions I have made, not as a prescription for you, but as a description of what one family does for alternatives.

One of the major decisions I made years ago was to get my son involved in a hobby that could also earn him some money and help him learn some transferable skills in life. CJ was eleven years old when I bought a woodturning lathe as the first step in an adventure of wood craft. A lathe is a tool that rotates a block of wood between two centers while the craftsman uses sharp tools to shape the wood from square to round followed with a variety of cuts to shape the wood into useful or decorative items. In our case, I taught my son how to make classic wooden toys, starting with spin tops and then moving on to other sellable items.

We successfully sold our products at a local farmers market for almost ten years. I would take my kids to the market every Saturday with only a few exceptions during the year. My son became an expert wood turner. He learned skills of interacting with people, while at the same time earning money and learning the value of hard work. I was proud of him for turning spindles to repair an antique rocker for a client who wanted to restore a family heirloom. Very few people today have the skills necessary for such a job.

That's not all, my three daughters also became woodworkers. My youngest was only nine years old when she began woodturning her own projects and joining us at the farmers market to help with sales. She's now eighteen and selling her products online. The same with her older sister.

I realize this is an unlikely fit for ninety-nine percent of families. It's not my intention to inspire you to start a wood working business, but I do want to inspire you to think of other activities you could get your family involved with that you can do together.

This woodworking endeavor has cost me more time, money, and energy than simply letting my children waste untold hours of their time playing video games or watching TV. I believe the beneficial results for my children were worth the sacrifices I made. I've worked alongside them, made my own projects, and funded our dedicated workshop and equipment with my own product sales. When the kids are all out of the house, I'll have a pretty sweet workshop to tinker around in! I'm not certain if any of my children will make a career of woodworking, but that was not the point from the beginning. The main idea was to give them something meaningful to occupy their time and help them learn transferable skills.

You might be thinking, *That's not an alternative to entertainment. That doesn't sound fun at all!* You're right, it hasn't always been fun, but it has been rewarding.

I mentioned in a previous chapter that my son and I spent many hours together building and flying electric remote-controlled airplanes. This is a great illustration for recreation because we literally re-created our remote-controlled planes more than we flew them. We did get better over time at keeping them up in the air, but this hobby is certainly not for the faint of heart.

My children all tend toward the creative side of the brain, so I have continually encouraged them to pursue other types of artistic expression and crafts. They've loved painting, drawing, creative lettering, ballet, and karate to name just a few of the activities my kids have been involved with. You and your children have a unique family DNA with your own unique gifts, unique quirks, unique limitations, and unique opportunities. Don't waste your limited time together as a family. Be purposeful and redeem as much as you can. The short-term convenience of screen time as a default may have long-term negative effects and consequences. Don't let digital media short-circuit more purposeful activities that can result in a better payoff in the long run.

Today's technologies should be viewed as powerful tools that require maturity and responsibility before handling. When my son CJ was a toddler, he was given a toy tool set and workbench made of wood. He couldn't get into much trouble or harm with play tools. Yet, as he started growing older, I wanted him to learn how to handle real tools and be able to use them effectively in real tasks. I didn't start by putting a powered circular saw in his hand. It started with a basic hammer and a screwdriver. He eventually learned to carefully use a hand saw. Now, as an adult, he works with power tools regularly in his job.

When he was younger, he became comfortable with using the wood lathe and a handful of other power tools. He eventually learned how to operate a table saw, one of the more dangerous tools in a woodshop. When he was starting out, I was not comfortable with him handling those tools without parental oversight and training. As he demonstrated wisdom and extreme safety in handling the less dangerous tools, I encouraged him to begin using the other tools that had greater risk.

The point I want to make is that parents should provide the same oversight and training when it comes to smartphones. I had no desire for my son to play with power tools in the workshop unsupervised with no purpose other than to amuse himself. When it comes to smartphones, computers, video games, and the internet, as a parent, you need to assess honestly if there is truly a beneficial purpose for these digital tools in your child's life at any given age.

Another parameter that I have adopted is supervised use. Going back to the woodshop illustration, I have spent innumerable hours in the shop with my older children teaching them how to handle the power tools carefully. I supervised them one hundred percent of the time at the beginning, and as they grew in their skills, I began letting them spend more time in the shop without me. My daughters still ask me to help them with some tasks because they recognize that there is greater danger if they do them by themselves.

Too many parents leave their children unsupervised regarding technology. They want it to occupy the child's time because it helps them to free up their own. It used to be that the TV was the proverbial electronic babysitter, but now there are a host of convenient sitters. The training your children need to enable them eventually to handle these powerful tools with wisdom requires your time. Your efforts are not a waste of your time; they are a worthy investment for your children and their future.

Here's some good news! Parental involvement makes a difference. Studies show that parents taking an active role in setting limitations in the home gives their children boundaries that they benefit from. Help them learn that these technologies are powerful tools that must be handled carefully, not toys for their amusement.

CHAPTER 20

RESTORING THE SOUL OF YOUR FAMILY IN THE DIGITAL AGE

Did you know that Gen Z is considered the loneliest generation? I recently saw the following quote in a news article: "People between the ages of 16 and 24, part of the group typically referred to as Generation Z, are the loneliest generation, according to new research."[1]

The fact that Gen Z is considered the loneliest generation may sound surprising because because young people have the greatest opportunity to connect with others 24/7 online like no other generation before them. Why are they so lonely? Social media was mentioned in the article as one of the culprits. These superficial connections do not meet the deepest needs of their life.

It is less surprising when we consider that today's digital connections are disembodied. You may be communicating with others but not in person, not face-to-face. Instantaneous communication between people who were not near one another was not even possible for most of history until the invention of the telegraph which allowed people to communicate simultaneously beyond earshot or eyesight for the first time.

I honestly believe that many youths and adults are finding themselves pixeled out and growing more aware of their need for personal change. Many feel trapped and helpless and are not sure how to find freedom. They are awakening to the need but unsure of the path ahead. Most importantly, some are beginning to see a possible correlation between their distracted lives and their distance from Christ and other important relationships.

Let me share a personal story with you. I was speaking to a group of teens several years ago in Knoxville, Tennessee, and afterwards a boy about twelve years old approached me and shared openly about the amount of time he was wasting playing video games. I was moved by his transparency as he explained his less-than-ideal family situation and gave some heartfelt insight as to why he was choosing the path he was on. He honestly stated, "I am lonely, and I don't know what to do with myself."

I believe he could be a spokesman for a large demographic of youth who mistakenly attempt to pacify their gnawing internal emptiness through a digital diet that can never satisfy them. Isaiah 55:2 says, "Why do you spend money for what is not bread, and your wages for what does not satisfy? Listen carefully to Me, and eat what is good, and let your soul delight itself in abundance." The souls of this current generation are lean.

They need a lighthouse to guide them safely into a peaceful harbor. They also need to see others who are demonstrating what it looks like to live a satisfied life with meaningful relationships starting with a relationship to God through Jesus Christ. Let's not forget that Jesus took on flesh and dwelt among people. He became embodied for us. I hope that you and I will be the examples that our children need, examples of what it means to follow Christ and grow deeper in our relationship with Him.

I began this book with an illustration from the move *Gremlins*. A similar analogy was made in the 1950's by pastor and author A.W. Tozer who was commenting on Psalm 4:4.

> "Commune with your own heart upon your bed and be still" is a wise and healing counsel, but how can it be followed in this day of the newspaper, the telephone, the radio, and the television? These modern playthings, like pet tiger cubs, have grown so large and dangerous that they threaten to devour us all. No spot is now safe from the world's intrusion…The need for solitude and quietness was never greater than it is today. Even the majority of Christians are so completely conformed to this present age that they, too, want things the way they are.—A.W. Tozer

I believe we can find wisdom from God's word. In the remainder of this chapter, I want to show you how Psalm 23 can help you and your family have restored souls in the digital age. It is a Psalm of King David, who worked faithfully as a shepherd long before he became a king. He draws from his experience as a shepherd to teach about his relationship with God and God's relationship to him.

Psalm 23:1
The LORD is my shepherd.

Who is leading your family? Social media and pop culture entertainment have an oversized influence in our lives today. The Lord should be the Shepherd of your home, not media and entertainment, not the philosophies, ideologies, and worldviews of the culture.

TV may seem to be outdated in comparison with the smartphone, but it is still an iconic symbol for electronic entertainment. The following parody of Psalm 23 was circulating around among Christians thirty years ago. It could be easily adapted for the smartphone today.

THE 23RD CHANNEL
(Author Unknown)

The TV is my shepherd;
my spiritual growth shall want.
It maketh me to sit down
and do nothing for His name's sake,
for it requireth all my spare time.

It keepeth me from doing my duty as a Christian,
for it presenteth so many good shows I must see.
It restoreth my knowledge of the things of the world,
and keepeth me from the study of God's word.

It leadeth me in the paths of apathy
and doing nothing for the Kingdom of God.
Yea, though I live to be one hundred,
I will keep on viewing my TV
as long as it shall work,
for it is my closest companion.

Its sound and its picture, they comfort me.
It presenteth entertainment before me

and keepeth me from doing
important things with my family.

It filleth my head with things that differ
from those set forth in the word of God.
Surely no good thing will come of my life,
for my TV leaveth me so little time
to do the will of God.

Thus I will dwell in the house of idleness
and slothfulness forever.

If we are not careful and discerning, we will allow technology and media to direct our lives instead of God. We will let it be the shepherd of our soul instead of God.

Psalm 23:1

I shall not want.

This part of the Psalm means being content, fulfilled, or satisfied. The analogy is from the sheep's need for food, water, and safety, but I don't believe King David was thinking only about his material needs. Like everyone else, David had deeper needs in his life besides food and water.

When your family is at the end of the all-you-can-eat media buffet, are your plates full but your souls empty? Are your children wandering in the digital wilderness and wondering if there's something more to life? Are you concerned that your children might be struggling to break free? Can they say confidently that their greatest needs in life are fulfilled by God?

Think about your own life, do you ever feel like you are running on empty? This might be physical, emotional, social, or spiritual emptiness. Do you ever feel like your spiritual fuel tank is on E? Have you ever felt that life doesn't seem to make sense, God seems so distant and removed from your experience, relationships in your life are strained, and there's something very comforting about zoning out as you binge watch a show or escape into a virtual world through gaming? Maybe you're a glutton for punishment by making yourself depressed by seeing what everyone else is posting on social media or getting lost for hours on end in the endless rabbit trails of YouTube videos out of boredom? Well, you're not alone. It's not just what other parents have experienced, it is also what your children may be experiencing. They may not know how to communicate to you about the emptiness they feel.

You are also not alone in feeling that gnawing emptiness when everything gets quiet on occasion, and you're not sure what to do with yourself. You're uncomfortable with stillness and quiet. You might be thinking, "How did you know?" I know because many of these things I'm describing are so common now, but many people are not looking for solutions for fear of others thinking they're weird or there's something wrong with them. The fact that you are reading this book is very hopeful! It's a step in the right direction.

I mentioned fuel tanks earlier and running on empty, so what does emptiness in our soul have to do with fuel? If you feel that you are running on empty, yet your life is inundated with a steady stream of screen time in various forms, it's time to start thinking deeper about how your screen time may be affecting you or robbing you of real fuel that you need in life when it comes to your physical, social, mental, and spiritual wellbeing.

If you think of media and entertainment as a type of fuel, and you are consuming lots of it, why do you suppose you still have that empty feeling? Because it's the wrong kind of fuel for the deepest needs of your life. Those needs are like a special engine that is sitting idle because it doesn't run on the fuel of digital media. The tank is empty, and you feel it.

As a parent, it's important to understand that the challenges young people are facing are not just what they are being exposed to, it is also what they are neglecting: quiet reflection, face-to-face friendships, beneficial outdoor activities, and the pursuit of God. Bibles are dusty, and phone screens are greasy with fingerprints from regular use. Prayer is forgotten or unknown altogether. Are you convinced yet that there is a need for helpful actions steps and hopeful solutions for the growing problems?

Entertainment and the use of today's tech do not satisfy; otherwise, people would put their devices down, but they don't. King David reminds us in Psalm 23 that when God is your shepherd, "I shall not want." He takes care of all your needs, not just your physical needs.

Psalm 23:2

He makes me lie down in green pastures.

According to Phillip Keller in his book, *A Shepherd Looks at Psalm 23*, sheep must be free from all fear before they will lie down and rest. They must be free from friction with one another, free from pests (flies and parasites), and free from hunger.

What does it mean for your family to lie down in green pastures? I've already given you an entire chapter on our need for sleep, which is being disrupted by screens. Late night entertainment and social media create anxiety not peace. They can open the door to digital pests that agitate. On top of that, the clash of opposing worldviews can also make you restless. King David wrote a similar line in Psalm 4:8 which says, "I will both lie down in peace, and sleep; For You alone, O LORD, make me dwell in safety." Peace and safety come from God, and your children need both to sleep well at night.

Besides sleep being disrupted, our children are lacking peace. Social media often works against peace; it doesn't provide good pasture for their wellbeing and lacks the protection from pests and predators. A flock of sheep without good pasture are always on their feet foraging for anything they can find to eat. Healthy pastures are not overeaten or filled with parasites. The more entertainment and social media that young people consume, the more trouble they experience. These are rarely green pastures.

A green pasture is a healthy pasture. Lush, nutrient rich, satisfying, and abundant. It is a good analogy of life to the fullest. Jesus taught about experiencing life to the fullest. He said in John 10:10 (NIV), "The thief comes only to steal and kill and destroy; I have come that they may have life and have it to the full."

Whether a good life is described as life to the full, abundant life, or green pastures, the important thing to know is that it comes from Christ. The entire scope of this book has been encouraging you to lead your children to something better than the current cultural norms, not to make life more difficult but to make it better.

Psalm 23:2
He leads me beside quiet waters.

Thirst is an indicator of the body's need for water. Your children have a thirst that transcends the physical. One of my favorite quotes is from Augustine in his first chapter of *Confessions* which says, "Thou hast made us for Thyself and our hearts are restless, till they rest in Thee."

A short passage from the prophet Jeremiah 2:13 can shed light on problems we are facing today. God says in Jeremiah 2:13, "For My people have committed two evils: They have forsaken Me, the fountain of living waters and hewn themselves cisterns—broken cisterns that can hold no water."

A cistern is a place in the ground for storing water. God said His people were trying to find meaning and purpose in life without Him, but it was like trying to store water in a broken storage tank; it just leaks out. God offered them a continual source of water, an analogy for real life in Him, the fountain of living waters, but they rejected their source of life. No relationship can thrive without regular and personal communication. Do your children see you continually turning to God for your needs?

Jesus satisfies our thirsty souls. We read in John 7:37-38, "Now on the last day, the great day of the feast, Jesus stood and cried out, saying, 'If anyone is thirsty, let him come to Me and drink. He who believes in Me, as the Scripture said, from his innermost being will flow rivers of living water.'"

Media and entertainment cannot satisfy this thirst. Owning the newest handheld technology doesn't satisfy this thirst. Only Christ can ultimately satisfy it. Jesus said to the woman at the well in John 4:14, "But whoever drinks of the water that I will give him shall never thirst; but the water that I will give him will become in him a well of water springing up to eternal life."

When it comes to our need today for quiet waters, be a role model for your children. Demonstrate stillness before God in your life. Let them witness the benefits of the still waters of Christ. Let them see you resting beside the quiet waters in God's Word and in prayer.

Psalm 23:3
He restores my soul.

Have you taken notice of all the latest news about the mental health crisis among teens? Studies continue to identify social media and screen time as the primary culprits. Other issues include sleep deprivation, the decline in in-person socialization, family instability, and the lack of physical activity and outdoor play. Many of these issues have been addressed already in this book.

Many people today are unaware that the word psyche (where we get the word psychology) comes from the Greek word psuche, which means the soul. Psychology means knowledge of the soul. God is the Creator of the human body as well as the soul. As the Creator, He is the foremost expert in the field of human psychology.

The Bible teaches where to find hope when our soul is troubled. Psalms 42:11 talks about the despair of the soul, "Why are you in despair, O my soul? And why have you become disturbed within me? Hope in God, for I shall yet praise Him, The help of my countenance and my God."

Some translations say, "Why are you cast down?" According to Phillip Keller, a cast sheep is one that is stuck on its back and can't get up. It's dangerous for sheep and can ultimately cause its death if not helped back on its feet.

Social media has caused a lot of cast sheep. You need to recognize when your children are cast down, in despair, and in need. Technology is not the answer. The Lord is the answer, and we need to lead our children to Him.

Psalm 23:3
*He guides me in the paths of
righteousness For His name's sake.*

There was a time in my life when I raised a small flock of sheep, and I learned firsthand that sheep will overgraze a pasture and ruin a field if you let them. They are creatures of habit and sometimes bad habits. They must be moved to better pastures when the field they are in is overgrazed or unhealthy.

The Bible often compares people with sheep, and like sheep, we also get ourselves into behavioral ruts. Your family needs a pasture rotation or to be led out into open range.

When the Bible teaches about righteousness, it is teaching about what is right as opposed to what is wrong. We need to let Jesus lead us in paths of righteousness. We need to discern between good and evil media and entertainment. The following passage uses an analogy of a baby who can drink only milk but should eventually mature and begin to eat solid foods. The analogy is applied to adults and can be helpful for parenting.

> For though by this time you ought to be teachers, you have need again for someone to teach you the elementary principles of the oracles of God, and you have come to need milk and not solid food. For everyone who partakes only of milk is not accustomed to the word of righteousness, for he is an infant. But solid food is for the mature, who because of practice have their senses trained to discern good and evil.—Hebrews 5:12-14

Christian maturity requires our senses to be trained to discern good and evil. As parents, to train our children is also part of our responsibilities. The verse started out with, "For though by this time you ought to be teachers." Our children do not learn how to discern good from evil by watching today's entertainment on screens. Much of today's entertainment teaches them the opposite.

I've already demonstrated in this book that one of our big problems today is consuming too much media and entertainment. It's not only about how much media and entertainment we are consuming, but what we are consuming. What is the content? Is it good or evil? Is it helping your children walk in the path of righteousness?

Psalm 23:4

Even though I walk through the valley of the shadow of death, I fear no evil, for You are with me.

For over two decades, I have been encouraging young people to commit to going on a media fast for the sake of their spiritual wellbeing. They often think that they are being led to the valley of the shadow of death if they decide to try a media fast. Your kids might say or think, "I can't do this," or "I'm going to die!" No, they won't die if they go on a media fast.

God is not leading us to the valley but through the valley because there is better pasture on the other side. I experienced the benefits when I went on a media fast for the first time at the age of seventeen. It was one of the best things I ever did for my spiritual growth as a new believer. Christ leads us through difficult circumstance for our growth and maturity. Remember that He is not leading your family to the valley of the shadow of death but through it because good comes out of the journey.

Psalm 23:4

Your rod and Your staff, they comfort me.

These words are a reminder that we are in a spiritual battle and there is an enemy after our souls. At the time when this Psalm was written, the rod was for defense of the sheep. It was also for discipline and could be used for inspecting the sheep.

The shepherd's staff was for the care and management of sheep, for their benefit. It was used to direct the sheep, to draw them to the shepherd, and to rescue them out of precarious situations.

Speaking of protection, let me give another warning against online predators. This threat is very real and another reason to watch over and guard your children carefully. Please avail yourself of the modern tools to help with your flock's protection. I'll mention again the Parent's Guide to Parental Control Apps in Appendix A of this book. Online predators are a real and growing threat to your children.

The church I attend is not a large congregation, but a child in our church fell victim to an online predator resulting in an abduction. Thankfully, she was found alive, though the perpetrator was not apprehended. It was a sobering wake up call to the families in our congregation.

God watches over His flock with His rod and staff, and parent's need to follow His example and be equipped to protect their children from today's threats by using modern tools and faithful oversight.

Psalm 23:5

*You prepare a table before
me in the presence of my enemies.*

Having regular mealtimes as a family is important. Jesus spent a lot of His time with the disciples around the table. In the 21st Century, we need to set some important boundaries and not let our devices disrupt our time of fellowship together. It's good to establish some phone-free zones. I know the verse says, "in the presence of my enemies," but the enemies weren't at the table. So, keep your phones in silent mode and ignore them or collect them in a basket while you are together. Try it sometime!

Psalm 23:5

*You have anointed my
head with oil; My cup overflows.*

We are taught by the apostle Paul in Galatians 5 to walk in the Spirit so we will not fulfil the lusts of the flesh. We need the anointing of the Holy Spirit in our life to help us produce the good fruit of the Holy Spirit listed in Galatians 5.

Our lives are often saturated with screen time which drains our cup and leaves us feeling empty. We need our cups to be filled and overflowing from the presence of God, not the screens of our smartphones. God is the one who fills your life with good, beneficial things.

The glow that people Israel could see on the face of Moses was from being in the presence of God, not from staring at a smartphone.

Psalm 23:6

*Surely goodness and lovingkindness
will follow me all the days of my life, And I will
dwell in the house of the LORD forever.*

Don't miss out on the blessings from the Lord. Allow Him to be the Shepherd of your family.

ENDNOTES

1   Future Care Capital, "Gen Z Are the Loneliest Generation, Research Finds - Future Care Capital," December 30, 2022, https://futurecarecapital.org.uk/latest/gen-z-are-the-loneliest-generation-research-finds/.

CHAPTER 21

HANDLE WITH CARE

The Associated Press reported the following, "Police say a frustrated Boston woman called 911 to say she couldn't get her 14-year-old son to stop playing video games and go to sleep. Police spokesman Officer Joe Zanoli said Monday the mother called for help around 2:30 a.m. Saturday to say that the teenager also walked around the house and turned on all the lights. Two officers who responded to the house persuaded the child to obey his mother. Zanoli says the mother's 911 call over video game obsession 'was a little unusual, but by no means is it surprising—especially in today's age when these kids play video games and computer games.' The Boston Herald first reported the 911 call, saying the boy was playing the popular Grand Theft Auto game."

After speaking at a church several years ago, the pastor's wife shared a story with me about their family taking a much-needed vacation. While on their road trip, their teen son spent most of his time playing a handheld video game in the backseat. Mom, who was in the front passenger's seat, asked her son multiple times to give it a break and enjoy the beautiful weather and scenery. He ignored her. She reacted in frustration, grabbed the gaming device out of her son's hand, and flung it out the open window. Her son gasped in disbelief, "Mom, I bought that with my own money!" She was unmoved by his protest.

I thought about giving her a high-five for being a proactive parent, but then I questioned myself if her response was the right action or not. Many parents could sympathize with her reaction even if there might have been a better response.

Conflicts about technology and media are common in families. We can all hope and pray they don't end in heartbreaking tragedy. I remember seeing in the news, "Iowa teen found dead days after running away in freezing weather when parents took away his phone." They were loving parents trying to do what was best, but this was not an expected outcome. Parenting is hard—probably the hardest thing you'll do in life.

In this chapter, I want to address the subject of handling conflicts with care. A single chapter is not sufficient for such a daunting topic, but I'll share a few essential principles that you may find helpful. I've been interacting with parents about media and technology for over twenty years, and I've witnessed how relationships can quickly descend from frustration to fragmentation.

SYMPTOMS OR ROOT PROBLEMS?

When I was a boy, my grandfather died of cancer. A tumor appeared on his neck and the doctors did what they thought was best to radiate it and remove it, but it kept growing. Eventually, the cancer and the treatment got the best of him. Cancer is awful.

Many years later, as an adult, I made a new friend at church named Peter. As I got to know him better, I learned that he was a cancer survivor. As he shared his story, it caught my attention when he talked about a tumor that appeared on his neck. He saw an oncologist who recommended radiating the tumor and removing it through surgery. His story sounded so similar to my grandfather's story.

In Peter's case, he felt led by God to get a second opinion. A different oncologist, who had dealt with similar cases ordered a biopsy behind his nose. Peter was taken aback. The doctor explained that it was possible the main problem was behind his nose and the tumor was being formed on his neck as a symptom but not the root problem. The biopsy proved the doctor's initial assessment, and the treatment that followed proved to be successful for Peter.

What I didn't mention before is that after my grandfather died, they did an autopsy and only then discovered that the root problem was cancer behind his nose.

I use this as an illustration to encourage you as a parent to make sure you are not just focusing on the symptoms that are surfacing in your home but are getting to the root problems if possible.

QUESTIONS TO ANSWER PRIOR TO ATTEMPTING CONFLICT RESOLUTION

Before you make any attempts to resolve conflicts in the home about your family's use of technology or media choices, it is helpful to answer some important questions first. I have five questions you should ask yourself and answer honestly.

QUESTION #1

How is your present relationship with Christ? If your answer is, "Well, not so great right now," it is likely that you are not in a place where you can be an effective catalyst for change and healing in your home. The well-known verses from James 4:7-8 says, "Therefore submit to God. Resist the devil and he will flee from you. Draw near to God and He will draw near to you." This reminds us that before you can resist the enemy's schemes, you must first be submitted to God. There is a real devil, and he wants disunity in the home. He tries to wreck everything good that God has made. Jesus said that a house divided against itself cannot stand. The opposite is also true: a house united stands strong.

Answering this question may be a catalyst for your own personal renewal in your relationship with God. Consider this advice as an opportunity to submit to God and draw near to Him. It may be the case that your family is struggling because you're not in the place you need to be spiritually. There's no time like the present to take the right step if you realize you've made some wrong ones along the way.

QUESTION #2

Have you prayed about the situation? Really prayed? I mean really, really prayed? I love the parable by Jesus about the woman and the unjust judge.

> Then He spoke a parable to them, that men always ought to pray and not lose heart, saying: "There was in a certain city a judge who did not fear God nor regard man. Now there was a widow in that city; and she came to him,

saying, 'Get justice for me from my adversary.' And he would not for a while; but afterward he said within himself, 'Though I do not fear God nor regard man, yet because this widow troubles me I will avenge her, lest by her continual coming she weary me.' Then the Lord said, "Hear what the unjust judge said. And shall God not avenge His own elect who cry out day and night to Him, though He bears long with them? I tell you that He will avenge them speedily. Nevertheless, when the Son of Man comes, will He really find faith on the earth?"—Luke 18:1-8

Asking God for help in your family should be ongoing. Don't give up if you've prayed before, and God doesn't seem to be answering. This parable is about not losing heart when you don't get an immediate answer to your prayers.

Prayer is foundational. We can learn about the importance of a good foundation by remembering the famous Leaning Tower of Pisa. Construction was started in AD 1173 as a church bell tower that would stand one hundred and eighty-three feet tall. It took one hundred and ninety-nine years to build at three different stages. The most surprising part of its history is that it began to lean while they were building the second floor. The reason was a shallow foundation made on unstable subsoil.

The builders tried to compensate for the lean so if you look closely at pictures, you might notice a slight banana shape to the tower. They kept building and the tower kept leaning. They should have started over after it first started to tilt. Unbelievably, the tower continued to move for several more centuries until it was about to topple. It was an engineering marvel that finally brought the tower to a reasonable angle. In 2008, the tower stopped shifting for the first time in its long history.

When the tower starts to lean in your family, stop and check your foundation. It's not too late even after you've begun building. That foundation is prayer.

A few years back, I shared a message about prayer with our congregation. I told them that five minutes of prayer is five times more powerful than no minutes of prayer. I believe we can do better than five minutes, but sometimes people need to take small steps forward. There was a problem with my statement, and my deficiency in the field of math became apparent when a ten-year-old boy corrected me after the service. He informed me that my prayer equation didn't make mathematical sense. He reminded me that five times zero is zero. Before you get irritated with the boy on my behalf, his next statement proved to be brilliant. He said that the correct way to make my point should be, "Five minutes of prayer is infinitely more powerful than no minutes of prayer." Not only is that statement mathematically correct, it is also spiritually profound.

QUESTION #3

Have you availed yourself of pastoral counsel to help with resolving conflict in your home? Reading a book like this one can be helpful, but it can't provide nuanced counsel in response to your unique situation. Hebrews 13:17 says, "Obey those who rule over you, and be submissive, for they watch out for your souls, as those who must give account. Let them do so with joy and not with grief, for that would be unprofitable for you."

Don't hesitate to make an appointment to get Biblical counsel from your pastor. If you are a member of a larger church, they often have multiple pastors on staff, so hopefully one of them can make the time to meet with you, pray with you, and give you some Biblical counsel for your particular situation.

QUESTION #4

Have you opened doors for your children to technology and media prematurely? Have you allowed habits and behaviors to be established in your home, and now you are frustrated with the results? You need to answer this important question before getting out the wrecking ball in your home. Where should you start if you need to reset? I asked this question to Bob Waliszewski in my documentary *Captivated*: *Finding Freedom in a Media Captive Culture*. Bob was the director of Plugged In at Focus on the Family at the time, and he recommended that you sit down for a family meeting and share something along these lines,

> I've made some mistakes in the past, first I want to ask your forgiveness, but from here on, we are going to make some changes in our home. And why? Because I want to be legalistic? No! Because I want to honor Christ, and I want you guys to honor Christ.

I asked the same question to Dr. Jeff Myers, the president of Summit Ministries, and he said,

> When you come home and say, "Kids, we're going to unplug because I've got all this new information here," there will be absolute warfare in most households. Why? Because the media has actually fostered an addiction. I would recommend, as a family, that you plan out a week

or two worth of activity, fun things that you can do outside. Just go play miniature golf, go play Frisbee golf, go play tennis, get some different things that you can do outside. But make sure you're together doing those things outside. The kids will probably be grumpy at first, that's okay. When you overcome an addiction, you're grumpy, that's just the way it is. If you could work through that for a few days and get a couple of weeks of being unplugged, you're going to find several things, in my experience. Number one, you are going to find that you actually talk, maybe for the first time, you really talk about things. Second of all, you're going to find a sense of peace in your home. Because rather than being a good way to vegetate and relax, media actually stimulates us in a lot of ways that really irritate our nervous systems. So, you're going to find a sense of peace. I think third of all, you're going to find that your kids are actually smarter too.

I also asked Dr. David Murray, a professor of Theology. He replied,

> You can't just suck technology out of your children's lives, something else is going to fill it, and it will be more technology unless you put something there instead, and show them the good things, the happy things, the beneficial things that can have that life-transforming and mind-transforming impact.

QUESTION #5

How is your relationship with your child otherwise? Meaning, if you were to remove the conflict about technology and media from the equation, is your relationship good and solid with your child? If your honest answer is negative, then there is a bigger issue that needs help before dealing with the technology issues. This probing question goes back to my earlier comments about root problems versus surface problems.

It's important to choose your battles wisely so that you don't fight a battle over technology and lose the hearts of your children. If you've lost their hearts, then fight for their hearts, not just behavioral changes.

A SHEPHERD, NOT JUST A FENCE BUILDER

I mentioned in the last chapter that I used to raise sheep. It was a small flock of about a dozen sheep on a small hobby farm. I must confess that I was not a real shepherd. A true shepherd lives with the sheep to keep watch over them and protect them. I just built strong fences to manage my flock. Building fences may be a good option for sheep but it's a terrible plan for raising kids. Not that you would literally try to raise your kids in a fenced pasture, but many parents try to rely on rules in the home without a commitment to being present in their children's lives.

The reality of being a shepherd without relying solely on fences was illustrated in what I observed when visiting Africa a few years back. Everywhere we traveled, we witnessed small flocks of animals grazing in open fields, in parks near the cities, or along roads. There were never any fences but there was always a shepherd or two keeping watch.

Rules are necessary in a home, and you may want to consider some new rules after reading this book. However, rules alone cannot compensate for a lack of your watchful presence in the home. Reconnect with your children. They may be drawn toward these other things because your heart and attention are distant from them.

It is clear that this generation of children are not figuring out how to handle media and technology with wisdom on their own. They are struggling, and so are the parents. Your children need your help, which means they also need you to show them how it's done.

Last summer, my wife and I enjoyed spending some time cooling off at a natural spring-fed swimming hole in our home state of Texas. We witnessed something becoming rarer, possibly on the endangered species list. It was a group of young children and teens experiencing the delight and thrill of jumping off a twelve-foot cliff into the water. Others were jumping wildly off a rope swing. I have little doubt that most of these kids had smartphones sitting on the shore somewhere among the towels and soda bottles. But for this rare moment in their lives, they were experiencing something the phone couldn't give them. Yes, you can find a number of videos online showing someone else jumping off a cliff into a swimming hole, but they could never replace the rush of actually jumping in yourself.

One boy, around twelve years old, was hesitant, fearful. We watched him get to the edge several times only to retreat. His friends encouraged him but to no avail. Then a little girl jumped in after watching her mom plunge into the swimming hole. I think her bravery may have finally convinced him, and he made himself overcome his fears and down he went. We didn't know him, but we were proud of him. Guess what? He climbed back to the top and jumped back in again and again and again.

You may be like that boy as you are reading this book and wondering if you have the courage to do something daring, like coming face-to-face with the mess the smartphone is making in your family. You've come to the edge a few times and chickened out because confronting the screen time issues seems too frightening. It may be helpful to know there are others who have taken the plunge and as their heads pop above the surface, you'll hear their enthusiasm, "You can do it!"

IN CONCLUSION

You and I both know that smartphones don't actually eat children. If they did, we might be more proactive as parents to watch over them more carefully and keep them safe. We certainly wouldn't leave them alone with a ravenously hungry smartphone, ready to consume our children as soon as we turned our backs or left the room.

The real problems arising from smartphones and other technologies and media are much more subtle and nuanced than child-eating devices. I've authored this book with the hope of inspiring you to help blaze a new trail and guide the next generation to learn how to use the smartphone and other digital tools carefully.

The hope is that our children will begin to develop reasonable convictions about using technology for good purposes while being savvy about avoiding the common pitfalls.

APPENDIX A

PARENT'S GUIDE TO PARENTAL CONTROL APPS

Parental control apps are essential tools for safeguarding children in the digital age. Below is an overview of popular parental control apps, their features, pros, and cons. Use this guide to consider the best app for your family's needs.

These are listed in alphabetical order. Be aware that new parental control apps are being developed as I write this, and others listed here may in time become outdated. I've created this guide as a tool to help you get started, be sure to do your own homework. Costs range from free to $50 per month with added discounts for annual plans.

Aura

Features: Content filtering, screen time control, safe gaming monitoring, real-time alerts, activity reports.

Pros: Integrates with identity theft protection; user-friendly.
Cons: No location tracking; higher price point; lacks social media monitoring.

Bark

Features: Monitors texts, social media, emails; web filtering; screen time management; real-time location tracking; detailed activity reports.

Pros: Comprehensive monitoring; unlimited devices; encourages open communication.

Cons: Limited real-time monitoring; potential for false alerts; can be bypassed by tech-savvy kids.

Boomerang

Features: Call/text monitoring (Android), app blocking, web filtering, screen time management.

Pros: Affordable; effective on Android.

Cons: Limited iOS support; visible app icon.

Circle

Features: Screen time management, web filtering, app blocking, location tracking, pause internet.

Pros: Comprehensive control; user-friendly; supports multiple platforms.

Cons: Subscription-based; limited Android compatibility; potential network performance issues.

Cons: Limited real-time monitoring; potential for false alerts; can be bypassed by tech-savvy kids.

ClevGuard

Features: Social media tracking, file monitoring, location tracking, keylogger.

Pros: Comprehensive; operates in stealth mode.

Cons: Expensive; limited iOS features; ethical concerns.

ESET

Features: App blocking, web filtering, location tracking, time management.

Pros: Affordable; user-friendly.

Cons: Android-only; lacks social media monitoring.

Eyezy

Features: Social media monitoring, keylogger, web/app blocking, screen recording.

Pros: Comprehensive monitoring; easy-to-use interface.

Cons: Requires jailbreaking/rooting; limited features on iOS.

FamiSafe

Features: Web filtering, location tracking, screen time control, driving safety reports.

Pros: Affordable; detailed activity reports.

Cons: Syncing delays; limited visibility into social media.

Google Family Link

Features: Screen time limits, app approvals, web filtering, location tracking, activity reports.

Pros: Free; integrated with Google services.

Cons: Basic monitoring features; limited to Google ecosystems; children can opt-out at age 13.

Kidslox

Features: App blocking, screen time limits, location tracking, content filtering.

Pros: Affordable; easy setup; customizable schedules.

Cons: Lacks advanced monitoring; occasional performance issues.

mSpy

Features: Call/text monitoring, social media tracking, keylogger, app blocking, location tracking.

Pros: Robust monitoring tools; operates in stealth mode.

Cons: Requires jailbreaking/rooting; ethical/legal concerns.

MMGuardian

Features: Call/text monitoring, web filtering, app control, real-time alerts.

Pros: Affordable; intuitive interface.

Cons: Detectable on devices; limited iOS functionality.

Net Nanny

Features: Real-time web filtering, location tracking, app blocking, YouTube monitoring.

Pros: Cross-platform; highly effective web filtering.

Cons: Expensive; limited social media tracking.

Norton Family

Features: Web filtering, screen time management, social media tracking, location tracking, activity reports.

Pros: Unlimited devices; affordable; easy setup.

Cons: Limited Mac/iOS support; lacks detailed social media monitoring.

OurPact

Features: App blocking, screen time scheduling, location tracking, screenshot monitoring.

Pros: User-friendly; cross-platform.

Cons: Delayed control implementation; limited web filtering.

Qustodio

Features: Screen time control, web filtering, location tracking, YouTube monitoring, app management.

Pros: Cross-platform compatibility; detailed reports.

Cons: Higher cost; limited iOS features; no stealth mode.

uMobix

Features: Call/text monitoring, social media tracking, GPS tracking, app blocking.

Pros: Real-time updates; stealth mode.

Cons: Expensive; limited iOS functionality.

APPENDIX B

PARENT'S GUIDE TO PORN ACCOUNTABILITY APPS

In my book Media Choices: Convictions or Compromise? I make the case that the best internet filter is the fear of the Lord. That doesn't mean porn filtering apps are not helpful or needed. It means that if there is not a fear of the Lord, the filters are limited. Accountability software and porn blockers provide fences, and they help police behaviors, but they cannot transform the heart. In the previous appendix I gave a list of parental control apps and some of them can be helpful for reporting and accountability.

The following accountability apps are designed to help individuals monitor and manage their online activities by providing reports to chosen accountability partners, fostering transparency, and promoting responsible internet use. Below is a synopsis of five notable accountability apps. Prices range from $11-17 per month with added discounts for annual plans. The following apps are listed in alphabetical order.

Accountable2You

Features:

Real-Time Monitoring: Provides instant alerts for objectionable content.

Comprehensive Reporting: Monitors internet browsing, app usage, and device activity.

Cross-Platform Support: Compatible with Windows, Mac, iOS, Android, Chrome, and Linux.

Pros:

Offers instant text alerts for immediate accountability. Includes location tracking and time limit alerts, beneficial for family use. More affordable compared to some competitors.

Cons:

Does not provide content filtering or blocking; focuses solely on accountability. Some users may find the interface less intuitive.

Covenant Eyes

Features:

Screen Accountability: Captures and analyzes screenshots to detect explicit content, sending reports to accountability partners.

Web Filtering: Blocks access to inappropriate websites.

Multiple Device Support: Compatible with Windows, Mac, iOS, and Android devices.

Pros:

Comprehensive monitoring across various platforms. Offers both accountability reporting and content filtering. Provides customer support via email, chat, and phone.

Cons:

Higher cost compared to some alternatives. Some users report that screenshots can be blurry, potentially leading to misinterpretations. Uninstallation requires a code, and the process may notify accountability partners.

Ever Accountable

Features:

Activity Monitoring: Tracks websites visited and app usage, including incognito modes.

Accountability Reports: Sends detailed reports to chosen partners.

Multiple Device Support: Available on Android, Chromebooks, iOS, Kindle, and Windows.

Pros:

Emphasis on user privacy with ISO 27000 certification for information security. Designed to be difficult to circumvent, enhancing reliability. User-friendly interface with high ratings on app stores.

Cons:

Does not include web filtering or blocking features. Primarily focuses on accountability rather than content restriction.

LeadMeNot

Features:

Activity Monitoring: Tracks browsing history and app usage.

Accountability Reports: Sends regular reports to selected partners.

Customizable Alerts: Allows users to set specific triggers for notifications.

Pros:

User-friendly design with straightforward setup. Customizable settings to cater to individual needs. Focuses on fostering open communication between users and accountability partners.

Cons:

Limited platform support; may not be available on all devices. Lacks content filtering or blocking capabilities. Relatively new in the market; fewer user reviews and testimonials.

Plucky

Features:

Web Filtering: Blocks access to predefined categories of websites.

Accountability Reporting: Provides logs of attempted access to blocked content.

Time Management: Allows scheduling of internet access to promote healthy usage habits.

Pros:

Combines content filtering with accountability features. Offers time management tools to help users control screen time. Simple installation and configuration process.

Cons:

May not support all devices or operating systems. Limited advanced features compared to other apps. Potential for users to find workarounds if not properly configured.

ABOUT THE AUTHOR

Phillip Telfer has spent over 30 years ministering to youth and families, speaking at camps, retreats, schools, conferences, and churches across the country. He is the president of Media Talk 101, a nonprofit ministry dedicated to encouraging wise media choices, and the author of *Media Choices: Convictions or Compromise?* and the young adult novel *Why Save Alexander*. Phillip wrote, produced, and co-directed the award-winning documentary *Captivated: Finding Freedom in a Media Captive Culture* and founded the annual Christian Worldview Film Festival.

Phillip loves Jesus, his family, and his local church. He serves as the teaching pastor at Living Water Fellowship in Bulverde, Texas, and is passionate about helping people grow in their relationship with Christ. Phillip and his wife, Mary, have been joyfully married for thirty-four years and are blessed with four children, two sons-in-law, a daughter-in-law, and four grandchildren. When he's not preaching, writing, or speaking, he can be found in his workshop crafting with wood or roasting coffee at home.

www.phelliptelfer.com

Scan for a free download of 7 Considerations in the Age of Video Games by Phillip Telfer

View this email in your browser

Helping you find balance and regain focus

Taming Tech: Tip #9

BE A GOOD ROLE MODEL

When it comes to taming tech, one of the biggest hills to climb is to become a good role model for your children. They need help navigating the digital age and you have the potential to be the best person to provide that guidance. Have you considered how much of their behavior reflects your own?

Young children and teens collect important cues about life through watching dad and mom. They may not consciously be thinking about mimicking your actions, but they pick things up for good or bad along the way. You are probably aware of the classic parenting proverb, "More is caught than taught."

Use this QR code to get more tips for taming tech in your inbox

Visit the Media Talk 101 YouTube Channel to watch the documentary Captivated

www.YouTube.com/@MediaTalk101

www.ingramcontent.com/pod-product-compliance
Lightning Source LLC
Chambersburg PA
CBHW020926090426
42736CB00010B/1055